Praise for *Distributed Leadership Matters*

"Alma Harris is a world leading writer on the thinking and practice of distributed leadership. This is undoubtedly the best book that she or anyone has yet written on the subject. Harris's view that distributed leadership is disciplined and collaborative counters critics who complain about the fuzziness of the idea. If you want a book that gives you an authoritative and accessible grounding, that sets out a strategy and a methodology, and that alerts you to the dark arts of distributed leadership as well as its payoffs when it is properly done, this is absolutely the book for you."

—Andy Hargreaves, Thomas More Brennan Chair in Education
Lynch School of Education Boston College, Boston, MA

"*Distributed Leadership Matters* is an outstanding contribution to the literature on real and enduring school improvement! The writing sparkles with inspirational examples of real-world leadership transformations that have benefitted staff and students alike. The research base is capacious and demonstrates the author's encyclopedic knowledge of school improvement and effectiveness from all around the world. Especially welcome is the crucial acknowledgement that distributed leadership can be abused and problematic if implemented in rushed mandates, autocratic rule, or mindless compliance. Here is a volume that will help us all to raise achievement with dignity. Here is a book that every educator can use to rally reluctant faculty, to focus on the instructional core, and to lift achievement. *Distributed Leadership Matters* is indispensable reading for every educator!"

—Dennis Shirley, Professor of Education
Lynch School of Education, Boston College, Boston, MA

"Leadership is a vision that is not held in the hands of one but in the eyes of all who are part of the system. This book allows us to see through those eyes and know what a collaborative unified environment does to make a school successful."

—Tania E. Dymkowski, Instructional Coach K–8
Hays Consolidated Independent School District, Buda, TX

"The book does make a unique contribution to the field of education because distributed leadership impacts leadership style and can guide leaders in moving away from traditional management techniques. Of great importance is the emphasis on the conscious and intentional application of strategies that reflect distributed leadership."

—Kathleen Ellwood, Assistant Principal
Irvington School, Portland, OR

"The author provides an eclectic mix of current research to convince educators that distributed leadership is an effective method to raise student achievement levels in innovative ways. The vehicle for this method is the structure and facilitation of PLCs. The author boldly provides a platform for difficult conversations regarding the challenges of this type of leadership and its effect on student achievement."

—*Laura Linde, Elementary/Mentor/Field Experience Coordinator*
Mankato Area Public Schools, Student Support Services Center, North Mankato, MN

"In addition to its readable and readily accessible style, this book's strengths lie in the discussion of the nature of distributed leadership, including the difficulties inherent in this form of leadership practice; the discussion around the relationship between distributed leadership, social capital and professional learning communities; and the discussion about building and facilitating strong collaborative teams."

—*Dr. Dan Archer, Independent Education Consultant*
Institute of Education, University of London, London, UK

"Certainly one of the most eminent scholars in the area of distributed leadership in schools, Alma Harris argues persuasively in her book that distributed leadership, in the form of collective expertise, carefully constructed through professional collaboration, can positively influence learning and teaching in schools. Drawing upon research findings and carefully written so that readers can follow her arguments systematically, this book is a valuable resource to readers hoping to find a reliable guide to link theories in distributed leadership to practices in schools."

—*Dr. Pak Tee Ng, Associate Dean, Leadership Learning Head and*
Associate Professor, Policy and Leadership Studies Academic Group
National Institute of Education, Nanyang Technological University, Republic of Singapore

"Alma Harris captures the essential challenges facing today's school and district leaders and summarizes, in precise and accessible language, important research-based lessons for practice. Her focus on building authentic relationships among all staff that will increase school effectiveness is both practical and a welcome antidote to an excessive focus on testing and standardization."

—*Karen Seashore, Regents Professor and Robert H. Beck Chair*
University of Minnesota, Minneapolis, MN

"Distributed Leadership signifies the cutting-edge development in the Theory Movement in understanding educational leadership, whereas 'professional learning community' is the most recent strand in understanding educational organizations. The book has successfully blended both concepts together and implied that they are the sides of a coin—not opposing forces, interacting to form a whole greater than either separate part; in effect, a dynamic system. The book is a must for most academics, researchers, policy makers, school practitioners and students of educational leadership, organizational study and school improvement."

—*Nicholas Sun-Keung Pang, Professor and Chairman, Department of Educational*
Administration and Policy, The Chinese University of Hong Kong, Hong Kong, China

Distributed Leadership Matters

Perspectives, Practicalities, and Potential

Alma Harris

CORWIN
A SAGE Company

CORWIN
A SAGE Company

FOR INFORMATION:

Corwin
A SAGE Company
2455 Teller Road
Thousand Oaks, California 91320
(800) 233-9936
www.corwin.com

SAGE Ltd.
1 Oliver's Yard
55 City Road
London, EC1Y 1SP
United Kingdom

SAGE Pvt. Ltd.
B 1/I 1 Mohan Cooperative Industrial Area
Mathura Road, New Delhi 110 044
India

SAGE Publications Asia-Pacific Pte. Ltd.
3 Church Street
#10–04 Samsung Hub
Singapore 049483

Acquisitions Editor: Arnis Burvikovs
Associate Editor: Desirée A. Bartlett
Editorial Assistant: Ariel Price
Production Editor: Amy Schroller
Copy Editor: Patrice J. Sutton
Typesetter: Hurix Systems Private Ltd.
Proofreader: Sarah J. Duffy
Indexer: Karen Wiley
Cover Designer: Michael Dubowe

Printed in the United States of America

A catalog record of this book is available from the Library of Congress.

ISBN 978-1-4129-8118-7

This book is printed on acid-free paper.

13 14 15 16 17 10 9 8 7 6 5 4 3 2 1

Contents

Preface

A great deal has been written about distributed leadership. Indeed there is a burgeoning literature on the subject. This is both encouraging and reassuring as the concept is now widely used and known. On the down side, some of the writing about distributed leadership has simply served to obscure a relatively simple and straightforward idea. Consequently, this book takes a realistic and pragmatic look at distributed leadership practice. It looks at the different *perspectives* associated with the idea; it considers the *practicalities* of making it happen and the *potential* of distributed leadership affecting organizational improvement. This book focuses on why distributed leadership matters, by looking at the facts, the evidence, and the practice.

Distributed leadership is primarily concerned with the interactions and the dynamics of leadership practice rather than a preoccupation with the formal roles and responsibilities traditionally associated with those "who lead." This book argues that it is the *practice* of leadership that is most important if the goal, in schools and districts, is to secure better instruction and improved learner outcomes. Most recently, Spillane and Coldren (2011) have suggested that the adoption of a distributed framework, under the right conditions, can contribute to organizational development. This is achieved particularly, rather than exclusively, through a process of diagnosis and design. But as the authors are careful to note,

> For this diagnostic and design work to bear fruit, in terms of student achievement and educational attainment, it must be anchored in the core work of schooling—classroom teaching and student learning leadership. (p. 108)

This book anchors distributed leadership in the core work of instruction and argues that to be most effective, leadership distribution has to be first and foremost focused upon improving learner outcomes. The chapters that follow explore and explain the potential of distributed leadership to secure improvement and change. However, as Spillane and Coldren (2011) note, people can exercise leadership but "fail to influence others to change" (p. 28). While this is certainly true, if leadership is defined as those activities or practices tied to "changing the core work of the organization" you would realistically expect to see some change in outcomes.

There are two important points to be made here. First, distributed leadership needs to be aligned to the "technical core" of learning and teaching if it is to really make a difference to learner outcomes. Second, to be most effective, the diagnostic and design elements associated with distributed leadership need to be firmly located within a clear, overarching model of professional collaboration and learning.

Even though the theory of distributed leadership is now well known and firmly established in the minds of those who think and write about leadership (Spillane, 2006) the important matter of *how* to make it happen is less well traversed territory. Accounts of distributed school leadership still tend toward theory, debate, discussion, ideological bias, and analysis rather than practical application. While theory is undoubtedly important as it can frame, explain, and predict, it is also important that theory connects, in some way, to practice.

This book proposes to make a direct contribution between theory and practice. It argues that distributed leadership is not just a powerful analytical frame or the latest leadership theory, but it is also a leadership approach that, if properly constructed and enacted in schools and districts, can result in better learner outcomes. The book proposes that, under the right conditions, distributed leadership can be a positive influence on organizational change and improvement.

Audience for the Book

This book will be of interest to practitioners, policy makers, and researchers who are committed to school and system improvement. It has been written for an international audience, and there are some specific examples to illustrate and illuminate some of the key ideas. In summary, this book will be useful to district and school administrators, district teacher coaches and teacher leaders, school leadership teams, professional development coordinators, and those teachers interested and engaged in the process of improvement.

Central Purpose of the Book

The central purpose of this book is to go beyond the theory by guiding readers to and through a research-based change process. The book links the idea of distributed leadership directly to *disciplined professional collaborative learning.*[1] The book's "big idea" is that distributed leadership, in the form of collective expertise, carefully constructed through professional collaboration, can positively influence learning and teaching. This book focuses on why distributed leadership matters, how it matters, and where it matters most of all.

Advance Organizer

This advance organizer offers a preview of what to expect in the book. It is an overview of the chapters and a summary of the key ideas. Essentially, the book is divided into eight chapters:

---

[1]See Harris and Jones (2012) for a full exposition.

- *An introduction and overview* of change, improvement, and system transformation (Chapters 1 and 2)
- *An analysis* of the leadership approaches and practices required in the future (Chapter 3)
- *An outline* of the research evidence about distributed leadership and organizational improvement (Chapter 4)
- *A commentary* on the more negative aspects of this leadership approach and how it can be misused and misrepresented (Chapter 5)
- *An analysis* of social capital—how to build it and sustain it for organizational change (Chapter 6)
- *A reflection* upon professional learning communities as a form of disciplined collaborative learning (Chapter 7)
- *A guide* to leading and facilitating or supporting professional collaboration with impact and concluding thoughts about distributed leadership (Chapter 8)
- *An Appendix* that offers practical resources that can be used by those leading professional collaboration

Chapters 1 and 2 set the global scene by looking at the challenges of educational change and focus on one key question: Why has there been *so much reform and so little change?* (Payne, 2008). Together, these chapters offer readers the contextual piece and advocate that leadership is *the* critical component in school and system improvement. For readers interested in the bigger picture, these two chapters provide a contemporary critique of school and system reform within an international context.

Chapter 3 looks at the type of leadership required in the future and builds a case for distributed leadership. It argues that future leadership from the corporate world to the world of education is characterized by collaboration, networking, and distributed forms of social influence. It highlights a tension between past and future leadership and argues that existing forms of leadership practice will struggle to remain relevant and useful in a global and 24/7-networked world.

Chapter 4 focuses on the *research* evidence and addresses the central question of *what type of leadership makes the maximum difference to organizational change and improvement?* This chapter presents the empirical facts.

Chapter 5 considers an issue that is very rarely discussed. It focuses on how distributed leadership could be misconstrued, abused, and misused. It considers the "dark side" of distributed leadership and focuses on what happens when things go wrong. Distributed leadership, or indeed any leadership practice, can be used for good or ill. As this chapter argues, much of the leadership literature tends toward the positive features of leadership, neatly side-stepping any references to the less favorable aspects. Consequently, this chapter looks at some of the more negative dimensions of distributed leadership.

The *how* of distributed leadership and the *practicality* of making it happen are addressed in Chapters 6, 7, and 8. Chapter 6 considers the relationship between distributed leadership and social capital. It focuses on how social capital contributes to organizational improvement and considers how it can be generated and sustained through professional collaboration.

Chapter 7 explores professional learning communities (PLCs) as one way of creating the structures for building the collective capacity for change. It notes that interpretations of PLCs wander between "whole-school" PLCs and "within-school" PLCs. The chapter proposes that viewing the whole school as an entire PLC is essentially *aspirational*; it is something to aim for, something that aligns with the broader vision or mission of the organization. In contrast, within-school PLCs are *functional*; they offer a structural mechanism for generating innovation and change.

Chapter 8 is written for those facilitating the professional learning of others. This chapter makes the case that distributed leadership can be enhanced, supported, and sustained through focused and disciplined professional collaboration (Harris & Jones, 2012). It introduces a *model and methodology*[2] of professional collaboration[3] for those working within schools and

---

[2]Further details about the disciplined collaboration model can be found in Jones (2013).
[3]See Appendix for templates and guides that can assist schools and districts in their collaborative work.

districts. It concludes by arguing that it is impossible to imagine how sustainable innovation and change in complex times can be secured without broad-based and sustained distributed leadership.

Collectively, the chapters are written for those working with and within schools. This is not a research book, although it draws upon the empirical evidence. The book proposes that if carefully planned and supported, distributed leadership can be a potentially powerful force for change.

Throughout this book, there are questions or points to consider that aim to do two things: first, to prompt focused reflection and, second, to highlight and reinforce the central argument and themes that run throughout the book. The last chapter is a deliberate departure from other chapters in the book as it provides a practical framework aimed at supporting professional collaboration in districts and schools.

It is easy to say that evidence suggests that distributed leadership matters, but in what way? It is important to reiterate that as each school and district is different, inevitably, distributed leadership will be different in each context and setting. This is not a convenient "opt out" clause but rather the recognition that there is no blueprint. Ultimately, distributed leadership will be dependent upon the individuals within an organization, their particular expertise, and the unique set of relational dynamics.

In his work, Jim Spillane talks about the importance of organizational routines and organizational tools that shape and define distributed leadership practice. But what sort of routines and tools best support the development of distributed leadership practice? This book argues that professional collaboration can be a powerful routine that effective organizations can deploy to support distributed leadership practice. At the end of the book, the relationship between professional collaboration and organizational improvement is revisited.

Should you read this book?

Think about the following questions:

- Are you committed to improving the learning outcomes of young people, whatever their context and whatever it takes?
- Do you believe that the key to school and system improvement resides in supporting teachers to be the very best they can be?
- Do you agree that collaborative learning with impact is achievable and sustainable?

The answers to these three questions lie at the heart of this book. The first question is about moral purpose, why we as educators do what we do in order to make a difference to young lives and life chances. The second question reinforces that teachers are not our best resource; they are in fact our *only* resource in securing better outcomes for young people. Teachers matter far more than they know. The third question implies that professional collaboration is one way in which we can achieve better teaching and learner outcomes. As I have said on many public stages, it is my belief that we have everything we need to improve our schools and districts *within them*—the real challenge is to make more powerful and effective professional connections.

There are those who will argue that this books falls into the trap of blindly asserting the normative merits of distributed leadership. Interestingly, when it comes to empirical fact, rather than ideological assertion, the dissenting voices are quieter. The idea that distributed leadership is "insidious" and a "profoundly political phenomenon" (Lumby, 2013) is to give distributed leadership characteristics it clearly cannot possess. Distributed leadership is nothing more than a way of thinking about leadership *as practice* and exploring how different patterns of influence can affect organizational change and improvement.

School leaders and district leaders understand, only too well, the challenges, potential pitfalls, and power dynamics associated with the redistribution of power and authority. There is no intention here to diminish the difficulties or to drown the dissenting voices but instead to outline the different perspectives, the various possibilities, and the potential that distributed leadership can bring to those leading schools and districts. Ultimately, these leaders will decide if distributed leadership stands or falls.

Engage with the Author

I hope that you enjoy reading this book. If any of you wish to explore the ideas further and to share your experiences of distributed leadership or collaborative learning, you can contact me at almaharris@almaharris.co.uk. You can also find more of my work at almaharris.co.uk.

Acknowledgments

I would like to acknowledge and thank the many educators in schools, districts, systems, and universities around the world who continue to influence my research and my writing. I would also like to thank and acknowledge a few special people who have contributed to the writing of this book, both directly and indirectly.

First, thanks to Michelle Jones, who is a constant source of support, creativity, and inspiration. Our work together with educators in Wales, England, Russia, Australia, Malaysia, and many other countries has been a pivotal influence on my thinking and writing. As a principal, with over twenty-two years' experience of leading at the school, district, and national levels, her mantra of "children first" ensures that our work together continues to focus on what matters most of all—securing success for every child in every setting.[4] It is a huge privilege to work, research, and write together. Her constructive advice and focused feedback on this latest book has been invaluable. I am also grateful for her permission to reproduce some of our work in the Appendix.

Second, my thanks to Jim Spillane who, without question, has influenced the educational leadership field in a significant and substantial way. His trailblazing scholarship on distributed

---

[4]Harris (2008), School Effectiveness Framework, Welsh Government.

leadership has shaped the contours of much of my writing, research, and thinking. His intellectual generosity and long-standing friendship has never wavered. He is a wonderful colleague and friend.

Last but certainly not least, I would like to acknowledge my sister, Angela Evans, who has worked in a primary school in South Wales for many years. She is an exceptionally gifted teacher with a talent for bringing out the best in all children. On a daily basis, she makes a difference to the lives and life chances of young people in ways I never could. She exemplifies what it means to be a true professional and to put heart into the classroom. Over my lifetime, she has unselfishly given her time and her love to our family. She makes those around her feel appreciated and valued. This is my opportunity to acknowledge her significant contribution to education and to personally say "thank you."

PUBLISHER'S ACKNOWLEDGMENTS

Corwin wishes to acknowledge the following peer reviewers for their editorial insight and guidance.

Dan Archer, Independent Education Consultant
Institute of Education, University of London
London, UK

Judy Brunner, Corwin Author and Consultant
Instructional Solutions Group and Missouri State University
Springfield, MO

Tania E. Dymkowski, Instructional Coach K–8
Hays Consolidated Independent School District
Buda, TX

Kathleen Ellwood, Assistant Principal
Irvington School
Portland, OR

Addie Gaines, Principal
Kirbyville R-VI School District
Kirbyville, MO

Bruce Haddix, Principal
Center Grove Elementary School
Greenwood, IN

Sandra Harris, Corwin Author and Director
Center for Doctoral Studies in Educational Leadership
Lamar University
Beaumont, TX

Mark Johnson, Principal
Kearney Public Schools
Kearney, NE

Mary Johnstone, Principal
Rabbit Creek Elementary School
Anchorage, AK

Laura Linde, Mentor and Field Experience Coordinator
Mankato Area Public Schools
North Mankato, MN

Tery J. Medina, Associate Director
The Southeastern Equity Center
Ft. Lauderdale, FL

Kim E. Vogel, Principal
Hood River County District
Parkdale, OR

For my mother, Marjorie Alma Harris
(1929–2010)

I hope I still make you proud.

About the Author

 **Alma Harris** is internationally known for her research and writing on educational leadership and school improvement. She started her career as a secondary school teacher in South Wales before moving into business development and starting her own company. After completing her PhD at the University of Bath, she held senior academic posts at the Open University, University of Nottingham, and University of Warwick. As professor of educational leadership at Warwick, she also held the post of director of the Institute of Education for four years. In 2009, she was appointed pro-director and professor of educational leadership at the Institute of Education, University of London.

During her career, Alma has worked with various governments and agencies around the world, supporting their school and system improvement work. In 2010 through to 2012, she was seconded to the Welsh Government as a senior policy adviser to assist with the process of systemwide reform which involved coleading the National Professional Learning

Communities program and developing a master's qualification for all newly qualified teachers. Her ongoing development work for the World Bank focuses on supporting schools in challenging contexts in Russia, working with a team from the Moscow Higher School of Economics.[5] She is also currently coleading the Disciplined Collaboration and Evaluation of Professional Learning program for the Australian Institute for Teaching and School Leadership.

Alma is president of the International Congress for School Effectiveness and School Improvement (see www.icsei.net/), which is an organization dedicated to quality and equity in education. At present, she is director of the Institute of Educational Leadership (see http://iel.um.edu.my/), University of Malaya, and is leading a major two-year research study focusing on leadership policy and leadership practice in Asia.

---

[5]National Research University, Higher School of Economics, Institute for Educational Studies.

Introduction

No country, however rich, can afford the waste of its human resources.

—Franklin Delano Roosevelt

A round the world, many education systems are seeking the holy grail of improving performance and raising standards. System improvement is now a common global aspiration and while interventions differ from country to country, the core purpose is one of securing better educational outcomes and better life chances for all young people (Hargreaves & Shirley, 2009). Over the past twenty years or so, the substantial school effectiveness and school improvement research base has clearly shown that *every* school, even those in the most challenging circumstances, can improve and, more importantly, sustain improvement (Harris et al., 2013; Chapman et al., 2012). This evidence base categorically shows that there is no ceiling on improvement and no limits on learning.

At the heart of my work is an absolute belief in success for every child in every setting and a resolute conviction that deprivation should not be, and cannot be, an excuse for educational underperformance. On a daily basis, schools and teachers prove again and again that the powerful link between poverty and underachievement can be broken. They demonstrate that every child, under the right conditions, can succeed irrespective of color, context, or culture. These educators show that success for every child in every setting is possible and whatever the sources of societal inequality, they can, with effort, be overcome.

As someone who came from an ordinary working-class family, I know that the combined forces of race, class, and poverty have little chance against a strong moral purpose coupled with educational excellence. Time and again, we see that education is a powerful force for good, for change, and for redressing divisions in society. It is this belief in the power of education to transform lives for the better that has led me, in my academic career, to ask why certain schools and school systems are more effective than others. It has led me to investigate the essential characteristics that make some schools improve, against all the toughest odds. It has also prompted me to explore the type of leadership that contributes to school and system improvement. This book, in part, is a response to such questions.

And answers are needed more than ever. Those leading schools and districts face testing and complex times beset by as many challenges as opportunities. The pressure to achieve better outcomes and to raise performance is stronger than ever. It seems that "raising the bar" is necessary but no longer sufficient. What is imperative is raising the bar again and again while simultaneously closing the inequality gap. In their work, Wilkson and Pickett (2009) demonstrate clearly why equal societies produce unequal outcomes. In their analysis, inequality is still strongly linked to a range of problems including mental illness, life expectancy, homicides, and imprisonment. Their work underlines that in an unequal society, however it is defined or delineated, by race, class, gender or religion, all people suffer, not just those who bear the main brunt of the inequity.

Their analysis clearly shows that the United States is one of the most unequal societies among those in the developed countries, with recent data showing that from "1993 to 2009 all growth in income was a function of the top 20 per cent of the population while the other four fifths experienced a net *decrease*" (Fullan, 2012, p. 73). Consequently, when thinking about educational improvement, particularly at the system level, it is important to recognize and understand the other factors that impinge upon achievement, performance, and outcomes. Educators can do only so much.

Despite this reality check, improvement is an expectation placed squarely on the shoulders of those leading schools and districts. This expectation, however, does not usually come with any guaranteed solution or any "surefire" blueprint for effective change. Instead, educational leaders are expected to find those improvement approaches and strategies that work or conversely are subjected to the interventions, programs invented by those often furthest away from the classroom.

In his book *Good to Great*, Jim Collins makes the point that success is not a function of circumstance but is largely a matter of conscious choice and *discipline*. A contemporary study of the top performing organizations in three sectors (business, health, and education) similarly underlines that high performance is a matter of choice coupled with focused and deliberate collaborative action (Hargreaves et al., 2010). The top FTSE companies recognize that their continued transformation is dependent upon the quality, nature, and stability of the interdependent relationships they establish. Staying at the top is no longer just a function of *individual capital*, that is, the quality of people hired, but rather is fundamentally determined by *social capital*, that is, the way the organization functions as a cohesive, productive unit or team (Hargreaves & Fullan, 2012).

In their efforts to raise educational performance, many countries are making the same fundamental mistake. They are focusing their efforts on securing human capital rather than generating social capital. In other words, they are paying much more attention to improving the individual performance of *some* staff members rather than investing in the continuous, collective improvement of *all* staff members. The top performing schools and educational systems around the world invest in collective professional capacity rather than individual expertise (Sahlberg, 2011). They ensure that their teachers continue to learn and are deeply engaged in collaborative professional learning. In short, the top performers are investing in social capital and collective professional learning (Harris et al., 2013).

In spite of all the evidence, many systems are still wedded to improving one district, one school, or one teacher at a time. This individualized, fragmented, and incremental approach to change is not only inherently slow but also unlikely to bring about lasting improvement, particularly at scale. It is increasingly clear that the only way to achieve large-scale and sustainable improvement is to invest in collective capacity building (Fullan, 2010a, 2010b). This means harnessing the professional skills and leadership capabilities of everyone in the system in order to improve the system. It means squeezing every last drop of collective professional expertise out of the system so that students achieve more and perform at the highest level irrespective of background or context.

This book focuses on distributed leadership as practice. It is primarily concerned with distributed leadership *with impact*. But let's be really clear. Collaborative or shared leadership is not the same as cozy consensus or unfocused cooperation. It is not about locating, reinforcing, or celebrating *sameness*. As Michael Fullan (2012, p. 27) points out, "Either too much sameness or too much scatter is problematic. Interacting only with the like-minded or being hyperlinked to scads of strangers is dysfunctional. Creative collaboration has a sweet spot that consists of the right mixture of established relationships and newcomers." Within this collaborative cocktail, distributed leadership is pivotally important because it is the "social glue" that supports effective interdependent working (Harris & Jones, 2012).

This book builds upon my previous work that has looked at the impact of distributed leadership on organizational improvement (e.g., Harris, 2008, 2009, 2010, 2012). But it is not just a rerun of greatest hits or simply a sequel. Unlike previous work, it argues, some would say quite controversially, that under the right conditions, distributed leadership can be a strategy for securing and sustaining better organizational outcomes. The emphasis here is the *right conditions*, not any conditions. It proposes that distributed leadership is not some random by-product of an effective organization but, conversely, can be a powerful contributory factor in improved organizational performance.

As noted earlier, there will be those in the academic world with pens already poised at the ready to argue that distributed leadership is some subtle means of control or conspiratorial plot or official orthodoxy imposed upon gullible, unsuspecting teachers. They will argue that distributed leadership is simply a more palatable way of handing out more of the load to those busy professionals who unsuspectingly and unwittingly buy into the idea. As Lumby (2013) notes:

> The resulting issues around distribution of power are largely ignored or referred to in passing; a kind of inclusivity which does not engage with, for example, issues of gender or ethnicity. It is suggested that opportunities to contribute to leadership are not equal and that distributed leadership remains silent on persistent structural barriers. The theory's confusions, contradictions and utopian depictions are argued to be a profoundly political phenomenon, replete with the uses and abuses of power. (p. 1)

Inevitably, issues of power, authority, and inequality loom over distributed leadership as they do in any other form of leadership and its associated practice. The aim of those writing about distributed leadership is certainly not to discount or airbrush out these important influences or aspects. Interestingly, despite several decades of leadership research and writing, issues of race, ethnicity, and gender are still not center stage within the field (Lumby & Coleman, 2007).

Consequently, while it is acknowledged that we need more empirical studies that address such issues, as the research base on distributed leadership matures, it is anticipated that there will be more empirical evidence to focus and inform such discussion.

Another critique focuses on the "strangeness of the rise of distributed leadership" (Hall, 2013 p. 1). The article states:

> Although the forms which distributed leadership takes within different school settings are in part shaped by particular contextual features within individual institutions the capacity of officially authorised discourses of distributed leadership to reach into the social practices of schools remains strong. Indeed, the very strangeness of the forms which distributed leadership takes in different institutions is shown to be intimately linked to the strength and intensity of this official discourse as designated school leaders and teachers seek to accommodate this notion into their practices. (Hall, 2013, p. 468)

First, I am not sure what "officially authorised discourses of distributed leadership" actually means. Second, I am unclear how they can have capacity. The argument in this article, and so many other articles just like it, is identical. Essentially, the conclusion is always the same—distributed leadership is nothing more than a manufactured construct imposed upon teachers and district leaders to subtly reinforce the status quo and to manipulate them into doing more work. It is an ideological rather than an empirically driven argument that assumes that those leading schools and school districts cannot judge for *themselves* whether distributed leadership is an idea worth their time or not. So in the pages that follow there is an emphasis on distributed leadership with the clear expectation that the ideas will be evaluated, considered, and assessed. They will be put to the test of practice. The core argument in this book is that distributed leadership, in the form of collaborative and interdependent professional practice, has the *potential* to contribute to school, district, and system improvement.

The book speaks directly to those in schools and districts. It makes no apology for drawing on the research evidence but steers away from fruitless and self-serving ideological debates. The first chapter sets the scene by considering the contemporary challenges and opportunities for school and district leaders in leading change in increasingly complex times.

1

Leading Educational Change and Improvement

No matter what states and districts do to bolster their educational workforce they will need to do more and better with the talent they have

(Darling-Hammond et al., 2009, p. 2)

In the relentless pursuit of improved educational performance and outcomes, there is preoccupation with finding new solutions, new ideas, and new approaches. It is as if we are starting at ground zero in our knowledge about educational change and improvement. Yet in our search for better educational systems, better schools, and better districts there *are* things that we categorically know. A substantial body of school effectiveness and school improvement research clearly points to the common characteristics and strategies that can be used to secure better organizational outcomes (Chapman et al., 2012; Harris & Chrispeels, 2009).

A far back as 1989, the seminal study by Susan Rozenholtz made it clear that the distinguishing feature of high performing districts compared to those performing less well is the quality of their relationships. She highlighted that superintendents that were "stuck" exhibited the norms of self-reliance and professional isolation. In contrast, the superintendents that were "moving" built effective teams and engaged in collective problem solving. The central message from this work and other more contemporary school improvement studies is crystal clear: collaborative working can be a powerful strategy if long-term improvement is the core aim.

Another clear message from the international research evidence is that *leadership* is a key driver in securing and sustaining improved outcomes (Harris et al., 2013; Chapman et al., 2012). Contemporary evidence points toward the importance of *instructional leadership* where the focus is upon emerging leaders and their ability to lead change that results in better learning outcomes (Robinson, Lloyd, & Rowe, 2008; Sofo et al., 2012). Instructional leadership is driven by the desire to understand the capacity of educational leaders to make substantial contributions to student outcomes specifically and to school improvement generally (Hallinger & Heck, 2009).

So do instructional leadership and distributed leadership actually relate? Yes, but the point of connection is rarely made. In their work, Heck and Hallinger (2010, p. 656) conceptualize instructional leadership as "an organisational property aimed at school improvement." As such, they talk about collaborative leadership or shared leadership aimed at school improvement, which encompasses "both formal and informal sources of leadership" (Sofo et al., 2012, p. 509). In essence, they are talking about distributed leadership. It seems that instructional leadership is little more than a shorthand way of describing those leadership influences and practices within an organization that impact upon student achievement. Distributed leadership is similarly concerned with the technical core of teaching and learning.

As Spillane and Coldren (2011) point out, "Even though factors beyond the school walls (e.g. students socio-economic status) do indeed influence student achievement, school leaders must focus on things they can leverage such as instruction. Thus connecting leadership and management practice with teaching and learning is essential" (p. 20). Consequently, instructional leadership and distributed leadership share more similarities than differences. The empirical research findings also point in a similar direction and reinforce that "collaborative leadership" or "leadership beyond the principal" has a powerful influence on instructional improvement and student achievement (Hallinger & Heck, 2010).

As educational leaders, at all levels, struggle with the many demands of their day jobs, it is important to highlight where ideas, research, and evidence reinforce each other and overlap. Unfortunately, some researchers in the leadership field are prone to demarcating, and indeed protecting, their favorite *leadership type*. The field is awash with "adjective overload" but simply putting a new word in front of *leadership* does not make anything new, interesting, or valid. What does passionate leadership, boundary-breaking leadership, creative leadership, or indeed any other type of leadership actually mean or add to our understanding of leadership or leadership practice? This pick and mix of leadership terms is simply not helpful to those in schools and districts faced with the daily task of making change happen. Therefore, throughout this book, the aim is not to make a special case for distributed leadership over any other leadership type. Instead, the intention is to stick to the facts, look at the evidence, and make connections.

But let's cut to the chase—what forms of leadership practices are now needed most by those leading schools and districts? The short answer is not the leadership we currently have.

For those leading schools, districts, and entire systems, the reality of improvement is messy, complicated, and emotionally frustrating. The pace of change, the pressures of the external climate, and the internal demands make it abundantly clear that the job of the school leader and district superintendent is now far too big for one. The expectations of those in leadership roles necessitate almost superhuman powers that relatively few mortals possess or indeed aspire to. The reality is that without actively and purposefully distributing leadership within the organization, long-term survival is not guaranteed. Without leadership, that involves the many rather than the few, those in formal leadership positions will continue to be vulnerable and exposed.

But let me be clear: distributed leadership is not the antidote to "command and control" leadership or a much misunderstood, misaligned, and misrepresented alternative to it. Rather, distributed leadership is conceptualized, here, as *shared influence* that can contribute to positive organizational improvement and change. In summary, distributed leadership is not just some accidental derivative of high performing organizations but rather has been shown to be an important contributor to organizational success and performance (Hargreaves et al., 2011; Harris, 2008).

Before accepting this argument, it is important to look at the facts. It is important to consider the evidence. Simply advocating or celebrating distributed leadership, without taking a long, hard look at the evidential base, would be ill advised and unwise. As highlighted earlier, the educational leadership field is prone to fads and fashions, sometimes with little empirical substantiation. Take a look in any bookstore, and you will see shelves of books on the topic of leadership. Discerning between commercialism, opportunism, and empirical fact is no easy task.

Consequently, this book examines the evidence about distributed leadership from various research fields. It devotes a full chapter to the "facts" about distributed leadership and highlights the contemporary evidence about the relationship between distributed leadership and improved organizational outcomes in three different sectors (Hargreaves et al., 2010). No apology is made for drawing extensively, and some might say exhaustively, upon the research evidence in order to explore the relationship between distributed leadership and organizational improvement. It is important that school, district, and system leaders know that any ideas or arguments made are grounded, have legitimacy, and have empirical support.

For those busy with the daily demands of running a school or working at the district level or seeking to improve the system, the question is, *does distributed leadership matter* and to what extent?

As well as taking full account of the research evidence, this book has been informed by the direct experience of leading professional collaboration in many countries, many districts, and many schools. It draws upon the work of coleading a national program of professional learning communities involving over 1,800 in Wales (Harris & Jones, 2010). It also draws upon a breadth of experience in developing custom-made professional collaborative programs in different countries: first, the "Teaching Schools" in England (Harris & Jones, 2012), second, a program for schools in high-poverty settings in Russia (Pinska et al., 2012), and third, schools in Australia that create intra- and interschool "disciplined professional collaboration" (Harris & Jones, 2012). This book reinforces the simple but profound idea that organizational outcomes improve if professionals collaborate in a purposeful and disciplined way.

Research has repeatedly shown that carefully constructed and disciplined professional collaboration can make a positive difference to organizational performance and outcomes. The emphasis here is upon the word *disciplined.* Too much of what passes for professional collaboration equates with loose or unfocused professional groupings, partnerships, or networks. While professional partnerships or networks have a variety of uses including knowledge and information sharing, the jury is still out on their ability to directly change learner outcomes for the better. An international review of school-to-school networks found that few could demonstrate a positive impact upon learners, particularly learner engagement and achievement (Bell et al., 2006). In their analysis of school networks, Hadfield and Chapman (2009, p. 9) note the difficulty of establishing any causal link between school-to-school networks and improved learner outcomes.

While there is no shortage of anecdotal evidence about the benefits of networks and networking, in reality, it is hard to substantiate any positive or lasting impact on learners. As some have argued, quite rightly, the challenge of gauging the impact of professional networks is difficult and complex. But difficult does not equate with impossible. Those advocating or leading professional networks have an obligation to find more robust and reliable methods of evaluating outcomes. Otherwise, why should busy professionals invest their time and participate?

The research also shows that to be most effective, professional networks require a certain leadership approach. As Hadfield and Chapman (2009, p. 153) conclude, for networking between schools to be most effective, there "needs to be a reconceptualization of educational leadership in terms of transferring knowledge, trust and shared purposes." As the pages that follow show, distributed leadership is characterized by high levels of trust, interdependence, reciprocal accountability, and shared purpose (Harris, 2008).

DISTRIBUTED LEADERSHIP

A great deal of the writing about distributed leadership, including my own, has focused upon definitional, methodological, and empirical issues. The question of how to distribute leadership has not had the same prominence. The few texts that actually tackle the issue of application tend toward description and, in some cases, low level and misguided prescription. While there may be some useful tips and suggestions contained within these ring binders and pages, grounded guidance to help schools and districts has not been so forthcoming.

It remains the case that the theory of distributed leadership is viewed primarily as an analytical device or tool (Spillane, Halverson, & Diamond, 2011). As a theory, it offers a way of understanding and interpreting leadership practice. There is no intention or desire to go beyond that to prediction or prescription. This is not a criticism but simply the case. Writers working with the theory of distributed leadership readily acknowledge that their intention is not to take a normative position or to speculate upon the potential benefits or limitations of this form of leadership (Spillane, 2006). Instead, they use distributed leadership as a lens or frame to investigate leadership practice and to assist leaders in the process of managing change (Spillane, 2011). While the theory of distributed leadership undoubtedly provides an important analytical tool, as Kurt Lewin said, "There is nothing as practical as a good theory." Plus there is emerging empirical evidence to suggest that distributed leadership is more than just a theoretical perspective.

Some have argued vociferously that the research on distributed leadership is still in its infancy, so it is really far too early to make any substantiated claims for it. Certainly, this is true, but only in part. While the evidence base encompasses a relatively short time span, in the grand scheme of things, it presents a consistent picture about the relationship between distributed leadership and organizational outcomes (Chapter 3). Also, do we really have to wait several more decades before utilizing and sharing what we know about distributed leadership practice?

While there are no "effect sizes" to give it the legitimacy and popularity afforded to other types of leadership (Robinson, Lloyd, & Rowe, 2008), the evidence base is growing, and most importantly, it is contemporary. While analyzing the research evidence, over ten or twenty-five years or more, is without doubt achieved only through exceptional scholarship, it is also critical to ensure that any findings are still relevant and applicable to the contemporary world of education. Schools are very different places from a few years ago, let alone ten or twenty-five years. So how do we know these ideas are the *best* things for schools and districts, not simply just the *latest* things?

Indeed, how do we know that distributed leadership is not just the latest leadership fad or fashion? The answer to this question resides in looking at the available empirical evidence and assessing what it reveals about distributed leadership and organizational improvement (see Chapter 3). While there are rare occasions when distributed leadership is a by-product of a particularly positive school culture, most usually it happens by careful design. As Leithwood et al. (2009a) propose, to be most effective, distributed leadership has to be carefully planned, supported, and aligned. In short, it has to be facilitated so that the best possible outcomes and results follow (see Chapter 8).

But before getting too far into the evidence base about distributed leadership, let's step back a little and locate it in the contemporary world of education. Let's take a look at the challenges of 21st century leadership practice, particularly the challenges of leading change and improvement at scale.

2

Leading System Reform

You can't be part of the solution when you are part of the problem

—Bakri Musa

At the system level, the heat is on. The pressure for better performance, higher achievement, and improved student outcomes is intensifying, largely because of international comparative performance data. The anxiety to improve performance, at the school, district, and system level, is acute. The preoccupation in staff rooms, superintendents' offices, and the corridors of political power is exactly the same. How do we raise student performance and improve student achievement? At best, these conversations are about improving the educational opportunities for all young people; at worse, they equate with tactics for raising test scores and manipulating outcome data.

Paradoxically within this debate, schools are both *the problem and the solution*. They are the problem because they are the central components of the system deemed to be under-performing; they are at the sharp end. Conversely, they are also the solution because the system cannot improve its over-all performance without them. In the frenzied rush toward improved scores and better international ratings, schools still play a critical and pivotal role.

It remains the case that, for the foreseeable future, inter-national comparisons of educational performance will preoc-cupy the minds of policy makers and politicians alike. For the top performing countries, simply staying at the top is what matters most of all, at all costs. For those countries further down the performance table, moving up the ladder is what matters whatever the cost. The characteristics of the *high performing* education systems are scrutinized, dissected, and overanalyzed in the vain hope of finding *the* key to unlocking better performance and improved outcomes.

Reports from commercial organizations are taken as gospel. They create false hope as they fuel a belief, however misplaced, that simply replicating the features of high per-forming education systems might be enough to secure a com-petitive advantage. The deep social and cultural differences that exist between countries are ignored or simply airbrushed out. The only game in town, it would appear, is improved outcomes, improved systems, and improved performance. Set firmly and centrally within the DNA of improved system performance is the quality of teachers and the quality of lead-ership. High performing systems invest systematically and heavily in both.

It remains the case that there is no single example of school, district, or system transformation without some change in leadership or leadership practice. The fact remains that in terms of a school's performance, leadership is sec-ond only to the influence of teaching and learning on stu-dent outcomes (Leithwood, Harris, & Hopkins, 2008). This knowledge, coupled with an ongoing international agenda for raising student achievement has resulted in a widespread call for significant improvements in leader preparation.

Local, state, and federal governments; education organizations; businesses; and foundations match that call with increased investments in leadership development. The return on this investment is highly variable and in some cases zero. Leadership development is undoubtedly important but only if it reinforces those leadership practices that actually make a difference, where it matters most, in the classroom.

So what type of leadership makes a difference? What type of leadership changes professional practice for the better? Most recently, a summary of research has provided "10 Strong Claims"[1] about effective school leadership. Two of these claims point directly to the importance of distributed leadership:

10 Strong Claims about Successful School Leadership

Claim 1: Headteachers[2] are the main source of leadership in their schools
Claim 2: There are eight key dimensions of successful leadership
Claim 3: Headteachers' values are key components in their success
Claim 4: Successful heads use the same basic leadership practices, but there is no single model for achieving success
Claim 5: Differences in context affect the nature, direction and pace of leadership actions
Claim 6: Heads contribute to student learning and achievement through a combination and accumulation of strategies and actions
Claim 7: There are three broad phases of leadership success
Claim 8: Heads grow and secure success by layering leadership strategies and actions
Claim 9: Successful heads distribute leadership progressively
Claim 10: The successful distribution of leadership depends on the establishment of trust

Source: Leithwood, Harris, and Hopkins (2008).

---

[1] www.almaharris.co.uk/files/10strongclaims.pdf.

[2] Principals.

This research study also highlighted that the principals who supported distributed leadership, in the high performing schools in this study, had the following features or characteristics:

- **Values and attitudes:** beliefs that people cared for their students and would work hard for their benefit if they were allowed to pursue objectives they were committed to
- **Disposition to trust:** experience of benefits derived from previous trusting relationships
- **Trustworthiness:** the extent to which others trusted them
- **Repeated acts of trust:** enabling the increasing distribution of leadership roles, responsibilities and accountabilities and broadening of stakeholder participation
- **Building and reinforcing individual relational**
- **Organisation trust:** through interactions, structures and strategies that demonstrated consistency in values and vision and resulted in success

Source: Leithwood et al. (2008, p. 17).

To what extent do you feel these characteristics or features are important?
To what extent do you as a leader exhibit these characteristics or features?

As highlighted earlier, with any research, including the evidence presented in this study, it is important for professionals to scrutinize and judge the evidence before accepting or taking any type of leadership at face value. While there is now a growing empirical base for distributed leadership, it is important for those leading schools or districts to use their own experience to put the latest leadership approach to the test of practice and to apply commonsense principles.

In his work, Fullan (2011b, p. 12) advocates the need to use "practice to get at the theory and more directly to use practice to discover strategies that work." He argues that "the creative premise for the change leader is not 'to think outside the box' but to get outside the box, taking your intelligent memory to other practical boxes to see what you can discover." The stance of learning from practice (i.e. your own and others') is certainly not new, but it has been overshadowed by the commercialization of education which fiercely reinforces that all good ideas come from outside. Frequently, these ideas come from consultants selling their "leadership expertise." The main point here is that learning from practice, learning from direct professional experience, is far more powerful and influential than any external input or advice (Chapter 7).

A study called *Where Good Ideas Come From* (Johnson, 2010) highlights that mostly good ideas come from inside. They come from *change leaders working collaboratively to solve problems.* It is hard to find a better operational definition of distributed leadership or a clearer exposition of why disciplined or focused professional collaboration is so crucially important to high performance.

HIGH PERFORMANCE: POTENTIAL AND PITFALLS

As we have seen from the "10 Strong Claims" high performance leadership depends on trust and mutual respect. Leaders in high performing schools have the ability to be resilient to any threat, to manage any change, and to deal with any unexpected event. They do this because they promote collaboration and teamwork. The distinguishing feature between top performing schools or districts and their less fortunate counterparts can be summarized as high degrees of social cohesion. Exceptional schools like other high performing organizations (Hargreaves et al., 2010) work like well-oiled machines. They are efficient, effective, but most of all, they are intimately connected. The success of "the best" is heavily dependent on the "rest," that is, they formulate and incentivize others to work collaboratively.

During 2009–2010, a transatlantic team of researchers undertook a contemporary study of high performing organizations in three sectors: business, sport, and education (Hargreaves et al., 2010). This study looked primarily but not exclusively at the leadership practices within organizations with exceptional performance, albeit at a particular moment in time. The Performance Beyond Expectations (PBE) study found that while the contexts differed greatly, as well as showing very clear demarcations between motivation and intent, there were also strong similarities between the high performing, or PBE, organizations.

This contemporary study found a high degree of internal social cohesion in the business, sport, and education sites, and it was this factor alone that set them apart from their competitors. In other words, the high performance leaders invested heavily in building strong relationships, sharing leadership with others, developing collaborative teams, and generating high levels of intraorganizational trust (Hargreaves et al., 2010). One of our cases, Tower Hamlets, a deprived district in inner-city London, had been significantly underperforming, In fact, it had, at one time, been one of the worse performing districts in England. But so much has changed. Tower Hamlets is now one of the highest performing districts in the country. So what happened in Tower Hamlets?

Did the community change?

Did the parents change?

Did school staff change?

Did the principals change?

Did the children change?

The short answer is no.

So what did make the difference? Put most simply, the schools in Tower Hamlets raised their performance significantly through a combination of collaboration and competition.

The schools worked together to raise their collective performance but were also highly competitive. They thrived on *competitive collaboration* as part of a strong allegiance to each other. Allegiance, according to Alan Boyle, who wrote the Tower Hamlet case study, is where there is a "genuine collective responsibility with full commitment to the cause" (Boyle, 2010, p. 18). Across a number of the high performing sites, there was strong internal allegiance and the conscious use of collaborative competition as a deliberate approach to outperform their nearest rivals and to stay way ahead of the game.

The PBE organizations only achieved such a high degree of success because those in formal leadership positions understood that distributing leadership carefully and wisely, through a team structure, would result in better performance and outcomes. While they didn't call it "distributed leadership," the PBE leaders in the study built powerful collaborative and competitive teams that connected vertical and lateral leadership in ways that consistently produced better results.

The PBE teams knew exactly what they had to accomplish; they had "stretch targets" and were motivated by internal competition and clear incentives. For example, in the international car manufacturing company Fiat, the leaders of certain teams were also the members of other teams; they were not only leaders but also followers. These teams cooperated to complete tasks and functioned as mini earning communities, generating new ideas as well as solving problems. In addition, the PBE organizations had strong records of growing leaders from within. They understood that succession planning was unnecessary if they generated their own leadership talent from the outset, deliberately, systematically, and sustainably. Consequently, those in junior positions were given leadership responsibility and opportunities from day one.

It is not just the structure of teams that keeps PBE organizations moving forward, as every organization has teams, but the vibrant nature of the teamwork itself. PBE organizations have cultures of creativity and risk taking. They allow and

encourage workers to have freedom and flexibility to innovate and play. Like Google, they allow staff dedicated time to
think, time to create, and time to innovate. They know that the
competitive edge will be retained only if there are new ideas
that translate into new products and new markets. Leaders of
organizations that perform beyond expectations keep people
with them; they build strong, cohesive, and high performing
teams where the reward is intrinsic.

Much of the literature on school, district, and system turnaround implies that this can be achieved only with sweeping
changes in the workforce. Improvements can be made only
if certain staff "get off the bus" (Collins, 2009). Interestingly,
many of our PBE organizations excelled and had even turned
around, with staff who had worked there for decades. The
study found that high performing leaders within PBE organizations generated fierce loyalty, particularly among those who
had become disaffected or who had lost their way. This loyalty, or allegiance, helped the PBE leaders to make quick and
difficult decisions without losing support. It also meant that
the organization was not distracted by the process of rede-
ploying or removing staff but rather was focused on maximiz-
ing the capabilities of all the staff they currently employed.

The research findings concerning school improvement
and school effectiveness reinforce what many practitioners
already know; there is no school improvement without
teacher improvement. Building the collective capability and
capacity of all staff is important (Chapter 5). But in the "race to
the top," what seems to matter most are shortcuts and quick
wins, rather than long-term, sustained professional engagement and improvement. So what are the practices, policies,
and leadership approaches of those education systems that
have sustained high performance?

HIGH PERFORMING EDUCATION SYSTEMS

Point 1. High performing education systems invest heavily
in the quality of teachers and teaching (Sahlberg, 2011). It is
this factor and this factor alone that has contributed to their

sustained high performance. The best education systems recognize that the "quality of an education system cannot outperform the quality of its teachers" (Mourshed et al., 2007, p. 16), so priority is placed on securing the best entrants into the profession and supporting them with the best forms of professional development. These systems reinforce that the only way to improve learner outcomes is to change what happens in the classroom. This is easy to say, but it is notoriously hard to do.

The many demands on teachers often make even the most enthusiastic member of staff unable to devote sufficient time to engage in innovation and change. Alternatively, there are still teachers who believe, as Dylan Wiliam suggests, that after they qualify they are "good to go" for the rest of their career without any further professional learning or development. For some teachers, professional learning is simply passing the time when attending a professional development day without any expectation that they might change their practice as a result. It is about getting through the day as painlessly as possible rather than engaging in new learning.

So how do we change what happens in classrooms, where it matters most of all?

How do we encourage teachers to move away from normative practice and do something new or different?

How do we get teachers to step out of their comfort zone and take some risks?

What form of leadership is required to support innovation and change?

How do we change professional development so that there is an expectation of a change or improvement in classroom practice?

We certainly need more disciplined improvement in schools rather than constant innovation unless the innovation is generated by professionals working together on real issues of teaching and learning that matter to them. Then, innovation equates with improvement. As the last chapter in this book shows, disciplined collaboration with impact has to be a prerequisite, not an afterthought of improved professional practice.

> Changing teachers' practice is not just a matter of capability, competence, or confidence. It is a matter of building regular opportunities within the system for teachers to routinely and naturally engage in activities to improve their practice and where there are opportunities to learn from other professionals within their school but also in other schools.

So if the solutions are staring us in the face, then why do many of the improvement initiatives, strategies, and interventions aimed at school, district, and system improvement make little, if any, difference to the performance and achievement of young people? So many of the changes intended to improve educational outcomes have simply not delivered. Despite considerable investment in education and numerous reforms, few systems perform consistently well over the long term.

In too many education systems, "significant numbers of schools are failing, even though it has been proved that a school system does not have to have bad schools" (Whelan, 2009, p. 11). It seems that there has been so "much reform but so little change" and that "after a couple of decades of being energetically reformed, most schools, especially the bottom tier schools, and most school systems seem to be pretty much the same kind of organization that they were at the beginning" (Payne, 2008, p. 4).

Despite decades of reform, what has really changed? The gap between the achievement of young people from affluent and less affluent backgrounds remains and in some countries is getting bigger. Failing schools are forced or mandated to improve only to return to normative performance once the resources and the punitive pressure are removed. High performing schools and those at the other end of the spectrum are divided by social, cultural, and economic differences that are not under their control. So why so much reform yet little change?

There are *three* main reasons. First, many approaches to reform and change are "top-down," imposed on schools without any attention to building adequate capacity or creating sufficient social capital for the change to work. The history of educational reform is littered with examples of failed initiatives that have suffered because of a lack of sufficient attention to the process of implementation. All change fosters resistance, but imposed change without an adequate implementation strategy will inevitably encounter debilitating opposition, particularly if those on the receiving end of the change are not clear about its purpose or the process of making it happen.

So the first lesson is to ensure that any change efforts are generated by those *within* the system, rather than being imposed from outside. It remains the case that most systems have everything they need to raise their performance within the system, but at school and district levels, better connections simply need to be made. Better links between professionals at all levels need to be created, crafted, and consolidated so that collective practical knowledge is effectively generated and shared.

Second, there has been an over-reliance on the "wrong drivers" for system reform (Fullan, 2011a). One of the wrong drivers is an over-reliance on external accountability to deliver results. Unfortunately, where there is intense pressure to improve results, governments will snatch at solutions and mandate initiatives that have blatantly failed elsewhere. In the desperate scramble to move schools and systems forward, policy makers, especially from those countries that have not been progressing, tend to select the wrong drivers.

In his work, Michael Fullan (2011b, p. 5) highlights four main drivers of school and system which are unlikely to make a difference:

- Accountability: using test results and teacher appraisal to reward or punish teachers and schools versus capacity building

- Individual teacher and leadership quality: promoting individual versus group solutions
- Technology: investing in it while assuming that the wonders of the digital world will carry the day versus instruction
- Fragmented strategies versus integrated or systemic strategies

The point here is not that these drivers are intrinsically wrong but that they should not be the lead drivers for school or system improvement. The four "right" drivers he suggests are

- capacity building,
- group work,
- pedagogy, and
- systemic solutions.

These drivers are likely to be more effective primarily because they work directly on changing the culture of school systems. In contrast, the wrong drivers alter structure, procedures, and other formal attributes of the system without touching the internal substance of reform. In short, they are less likely to succeed.

The second lesson therefore is one about *capacity* building. It points out the need to ensure that at the system and school level, there is sufficient expertise, energy, and resource in place to actually deliver. Later chapters focus on what it means to build the collective capacity for change and what actions need to be taken to purposefully build social capital for improvement at the school, district, and system level (Chapter 5). But let's return to the characteristics of high performance.

The research evidence shows that high performing schools and systems balance pressure and support; they empower people to perform while holding them accountable for performance (Sahlberg, 2011). High performing systems tend not to set quantitative targets or publish comparative performance data; they focus on securing equity and excellence. The Finnish education system has no private schools and over many years has ensured that its public schools perform at the highest level; it invests in equity and excellence. There is also a history of investing in teacher research and forms of collaboration and networking that significantly enhanced teachers' professional practice (Sahlberg, 2011). Teachers are encouraged to think differently, to challenge, and to be innovative.

In direct contrast, the weaknesses associated with standardized reform are now becoming increasingly clear. The gap between the achievement of those in poverty and those more affluent students is actually getting bigger in the United States and in some other Western countries. Improvement is much more likely in systems that are supported rather than punished and where there is a concerted effort to support and motivate educators rather than rely on simple accountability measures to ratchet up their performance.

A third reason for the failure of so much top-down reform is the reckless and often unprincipled *speed* of change. The overarching and compulsive desire for immediate gains, often politically motivated, results in changes being introduced at a sprinting pace, sometimes before there is sufficient evidence to suggest that scaling up is desirable or sensible or realistic! As a result, the conveyor belt of new innovations, interventions, and initiatives keeps policy makers busy but often unproductively so. The preoccupation with securing change, any sort of change—is much more important than thinking about "who is the change for?"

The automatic response to this question is that the change is for young people. It is intended to improve the system so all learners can achieve more and fulfill their ambitions. We would all applaud this. But in reality, the reform processes that are deployed often do not serve the needs of children first or well. In many cases, there is insufficient in-depth consideration of exactly *how* the policies will impact upon young people, their life chances, their well-being, and their learning. So lesson number three is to look at "what works" in changing schools for the better irrespective of context or culture or political expediency.

What Works?

Looking at the best performing education systems around the world, like Finland, Singapore, Hong Kong, and Shanghai, there is one consistent and powerful common denominator. They all invest in teachers' professional learning and heavily subscribe to models of systematic professional collaboration (Jensen et al., 2012). In Finland, teachers have dedicated time during the school week to work and learn together (Sahlberg, 2011). In Singapore, teachers are viewed as partners in reform (Jensen et al., 2012). Teacher inquiry groups are a consistent and dominant feature of professional learning and are a key strategy of improvement at scale. Teachers engage in "active professional collaboration that has a direct impact on teaching and learning" (Jensen et al., 2012, p. 16).

In Hong Kong, professional learning communities and district-level clusters are being developed to enable teachers to learn from others' experiences and reinforce effective implementation within schools. Curriculum team leaders are assigned to each key learning area to oversee how reforms were implemented in their schools. These curriculum team leaders are the champions of effective implementation of new pedagogy (Jensen et al., 2012, p. 37).

In Shanghai, teachers engage in lesson study as a core component of their professional development requirements and actively work with other teachers to develop new materials, resources, and insights. The teachers are put into research and lesson groups, and they meet in networks in and between schools. Teachers are viewed as researchers who lead reform and implement new pedagogy. In Shanghai, teachers' professional learning emphasizes high-level research by teachers. To become an advanced teacher, a teacher has to have one of their published papers reviewed by an expert committee.

In summary, the top performing education systems have embraced the power of focused or disciplined professional collaboration. They do everything they can to support teachers and teachers' professional learning. The focus is on *learning* not *teaching*. This difference is subtle but important because "it puts greater focus on assessing student learning outcomes rather than assessing teachers" (Jensen et al., 2012, p. 17). A focus on learning rather than on teaching increases the status of teachers as it highlights the complexity of the learning process. It reinforces the recognition that to be a teacher requires expertise and knowledge about learning theory and effective instructional practice. It signals that teaching demands a high level of skill, knowledge, and expertise.

> Essentially, to be a teacher commands respect because "it is complex, requiring theory and practice to be brought together by true professionals" (Jensen et al., 2012, p. 23).

One of the hallmarks of educational excellence and success is the nature and extent of professional collaboration. As the high performing systems show, focused and systematic collaboration can be a powerful influence upon changing and improving professional practice. When the vast amount of writing and research dedicated to leadership is analyzed and synthesized, what the most effective leaders do is to engage in and support the *professional learning of others* (Robinson Lloyd, and Rowe, 2008).

Effective leaders understand that when professionals collaborate with others on real rather than perceived or contrived issues, problems, or challenges that matter to them, the potential for learning can be quite dramatic. For example, in Hong Kong, principals play a key role in the implementation of changed pedagogy. They ensure that the professional learning and the development of teachers is aligned and appropriate to secure positive changes in the classroom. So professional collaboration is important in seeking and securing higher performance—but here comes an important "health warning." Do not confuse collaboration with cooperation.

To Collaborate or Cooperate?

This question is not just an issue of semantics. So much of what passes for professional collaboration, in the form of networks, partnerships, action learning sets, or professional learning communities, equates with little more than loose cooperation. It is simply professionals working together to disseminate information or to share good practice. Even though one of the advocated benefits of professional networking is "sharing good practice," in reality, this can sometimes equate with low-level "story swapping." As David Hargreaves (2010) points out, "Most sharing of good practice does not amount to practice transfer, unless the practice is very simple. As one of the major means of improving teaching and learning, it is a relative *failure*" (p. 4).

The whole point of professional collaborative learning is to generate new practices, ideas, and knowledge. It is to engage in focused collaboration that will ultimately push the boundaries of professional learning. It is not about reprocessing or rebranding tired old ideas. Recycled or reconstituted knowledge may be comforting and even reassuring to some, but it is unlikely to change or transform practice. If professionals actively learn with and from each other in a constructive and rigorous way, then a positive influence upon practice is much more likely.

Cooperation may masquerade as collaboration, as essentially it looks the same. For example, simply putting children into groups might foster cooperation, but it doesn't guarantee collaboration. The same is true for adults. Also, the outcomes from cooperation versus collaboration differ quite substantially. Evidence from a recent meta-analysis has shown that compared with individualistic or competitive learning, collaborative learning has very powerful effects on achievement. It also shows that while cooperation can reinforce positive social relationships, there is limited evidence of improved outcomes (Johnson & Johnson, 2010). So where professionals work collectively and systematically, when they engage in systematic or disciplined collaboration, then positive outcomes are much more likely to result.

To what extent do those within your organization collaborate as a team or just cooperate as a set of individuals?

So to return to distributed leadership, it comes down to one thing and one thing only—*how influence is shared.* Distributed leadership implies that successful leadership is not simply a function of what superintendents do in districts or what principals or assistant principals do in schools. It is the quality of their relationships and interactions that matter. In essence, distributed leadership involves the practices of multiple individuals and occurs through the complex network of relationships and interactions among all staff members (Spillane, Halverson, & Diamond, 2001a).

As highlighted earlier, this book is aimed primarily but not exclusively at those charged with improving performance and outcomes at the school, district, and system levels. It is intended to guide and inform the thinking and action of those who facilitate the professional learning of others in schools, districts, and school systems. It is intended for educational leaders, at all levels, who are leaders for the future and not just managers of the past. The next chapter considers future leadership.

3

Future
Leadership

As we look ahead into the next century, leaders will be those who empower others.

— Bill Gates

I f you think about your school or district, I can guarantee that you experience a constant tension. A tension between knowing what is important for the future versus managing the pressures of the present. So often I hear the comment, "I agree with distributed leadership, but how can it be fitted into our existing system? It's simply not going to work with the structures that we have." Usually, I don't respond directly to the question. Not because I don't have an answer but because it is the wrong question. It's like asking how to fit a Porsche engine into a tractor. The real question should be, what type of leadership do we need to secure the best outcomes for young people, and how do we change our structures to make this happen?

If the existing leadership approaches are not securing the best outcomes, then why should we want to keep them? But the fact is, we do retain those leadership practices that are not working, sometimes with a vengeance. The reason for keeping them, so often, is because it will be difficult, disruptive, and debilitating to change them, plus there is no guarantee of success if we introduce alternative ways of working. True. But keeping things the way they are isn't any guarantee of success either. In fact, it's a certain way to hold back progress. In the natural world, the absence of change means one thing and one thing only: extinction. In the corporate world, hanging on to old structures means giving the competition a major advantage. Yet in education, retaining the existing ways of working is tinged with a heavy dose of nostalgia. Custom and tradition are used to rationalize continual investment in practices that are no longer fit for purpose. But the world is changing, learning is changing, and so should leadership.

The status quo is simply not an option. In their book *The Fourth Way,* Andy Hargreaves and Dennis Shirley clearly and compellingly outline the principles of future educational change. They reinforce that within the "fourth way," teachers set their own shared targets, rather than scurrying around to meet the targets demanded by others. In the fourth way, democracy plus professionalism replaces bureaucracy and the market; it is less about government and more about empowerment. Finally, responsibility and leadership come before accountability because it is recognized that ultimately, it is collective responsibility and distributed leadership that will lift the system.

The Fourth Way underscores the need for professional learning communities (PLCs) within, between, and across schools that are dedicated to improving the learning of students and adults alike. However, Hargreaves and Shirley caution that teacher collaboration in the form of professional learning communities (Chapter 7) that concentrate on *raising test scores alone* rather than inspiring focused professional discussion about *students' learning* are likely to be less effective. They argue that the best professional collaborative learning, in the form of PLCs, transforms instruction so that it subsequently impacts upon results.

Professional collaboration can occur in the form of professional learning communities and other team configurations, but unless there is *disciplined inquiry* at the core of collaborative professional learning, it is unlikely to make a difference to learner outcomes (Harris & Jones 2012).

In the future, learners will need to be much more responsive to a rapidly changing environment and set of circumstances. They will need to be *highly adaptable* and responsive to shifting needs and priorities. Therefore, the leadership practice or practices within the school, or whatever the learning space will be called in the future, will also have to be adaptive, flexible, and highly responsive to external and internal changes. This will necessitate a shift away from vertical, top-down, imposed change to *lateral and collective capacity building* where collaborative professional learning is an integral component of better performance. Or to highlight the point, it is where past or existing leadership practice is replaced with future leadership practice:

Past Leadership	Future Leadership
Hierarchical and Fixed	Lateral and Distributed
Role and Position	Talent and Capability
Located in One School	Movement Around Schools
Problem Based	Solution Focused
Skills	Practice
Control and Efficiency	Capacity Building and Relational Capital
Focused on Organization	Focused on Instruction
Linked to Remuneration	Linked to Professional Growth

The intention here is not to polarize one type of leadership as good or bad but to try to look at the ways in which leadership can become aligned more closely to the emerging reality and future demands of 21st century education.

> Think about your context: how far is leadership practice "past" or "future"?
>
> What are the implications of the current nature of leadership for you and your organization?

In his book *The Wisdom of Crowds,* James Surowiecki (2005) argues that "diversity helps because it actually adds perspectives that would otherwise be absent" (p. 29). This suggests that the potential for imaginative and creative solutions to problems is more likely to occur where there is *diversity* of leadership practice that fits the contours or the needs of the organization or system.

Two decades ago, Ron Heifetz (1994) formulated the idea of an adaptive challenge where solutions lie outside the current way of operating. It is clear that the leadership we now require is outside our current way of operating and that essentially to be more adaptive and responsive will require much greater leadership capacity and capability. This will require leadership that is distributed across the community in its widest and most diverse sense. It will require the following:

- Leadership that crosses structural, cultural, and personal barriers
- Leadership that builds capacity within schools, communities, and systems
- Leadership that generates relational and social capital
- Leadership that sustains performance
- Leadership that supports redesign and self-renewal

But there is an important fault line. Despite knowing and accepting that we need new approaches to leadership, many schools and districts are still perpetuating past models of practice. They continue to provide safe, conventional leadership solutions to complex leadership problems. They are still wedded to the seductive idea of the individual leader, the charismatic leader, and the all-powerful principal or superintendent who will rescue the organization and turn things around.

While there is nothing inherently wrong with charismatic leadership, the problem is that these leaders come in relatively short supply and most schools or districts cannot wait for the "right" leader to ride over the hill. So rather than waiting for the right individual, the question is, why not tap and realize all the leadership potential that already exists within the organization?

Where is the untapped leadership potential in your organization?

How far are you developing the leadership capability of others?

To what extent are those without formal leadership responsibility being given the opportunity to lead?

In his book *Cognition in the Wild*, Edward Hutchings talks about the forms of effective communication and learning with a large and complex organization—a naval ship. His basic premise is that the ship functions as a large but highly effective learning community, collectively solving problems through shared expertise and knowledge. The interdependence of the individual and the environment means that human activity is *distributed in the interactive web of actors, artifacts, and the situation* (Spillane, 2006). This distributed cognition is what Hutchings equates with *effective system learning*.

While the world of a 21st century schooling may be very different from that of a naval ship, they are both highly complex social systems that require distributed leadership to function most effectively. Distributed leadership underlines the importance of collective knowledge and understanding. It emphasizes that leadership in complex systems can be *distributed and shared* only if real and authentic learning is to take place. But what is meant by distributed leadership and what difference does it actually make?

DISTRIBUTED LEADERSHIP

In one sense, all leadership is distributed. If leadership equates with influence, it will be experienced at different levels and different points within any organization. However, to understand distributed leadership, beyond an overly simplistic notion of just dividing up the leadership responsibilities or simply delegating more routine tasks, means highlighting a number of important features that distinguish this type of leadership from other forms.

In essence, distributed leadership is best understood as "practice distributed over leaders, followers and their situation and incorporates the activities of multiple groups of individuals" (Spillane, 2006, p.12). This implies a social distribution of leadership where the leadership function is "stretched over the work of a number of individuals and the task is accomplished through the interaction of multiple leaders" (Spillane, Halverson, & Diamond, 2001b, pp. 23–28). This theoretical framing implies that the social context, and the interrelationships therein, is an integral part of the leadership activity and implies that leadership is *broad-based, stretched,* and *extended* within, across, and between schools (Harris, 2008).

Distributed leadership is concerned with two things:

- *The process of leadership*—how leadership practice occurs within the organization
- *Leadership activity*—how leadership is enhanced, extended, and developed

Distributed leadership is primarily concerned with mobilizing leadership expertise at all levels in the organization to generate more opportunities for change and to generate the capacity for improvement. The emphasis is upon *interdependent interaction and practice* rather than *individual and independent actions* associated with those with formal leadership roles or responsibilities.

To summarize,

- distributed leadership is concerned with building the capacity to innovate and change;
- distributed leadership is inclusive and implies broad-based involvement in leadership practice;
- distributed leadership does not mean everybody leads but rather that everybody has the potential to lead, at some time, depending on expertise and experience;
- distributed leadership occurs in various patterns—there is no overall blueprint—it depends on the context but it requires planning and alignment;
- distributed leadership requires high levels of trust and reciprocal learning.

In very practical terms, to be most effective, distributed leadership has to be carefully planned and deliberately orchestrated. It won't just happen. Therefore, those in formal leadership roles have a key role to play in creating the conditions for distributed leadership to occur. They are responsible for making it happen. Formal leaders have to model distributed leadership by actively encouraging others to take the lead, at appropriate times. They need to invite others to lead and to reinforce the idea that leadership is about expertise as well as responsibility. They have to facilitate the professional collaboration of others (Chapter 8).

Those in formal leadership roles also need to consider whether their school or district is ready for distributed leadership. So, for example, if your school or district is in crisis or turmoil, is under external scrutiny or external control, then introducing or extending distributed leadership further is not a sensible option. Similarly, if there are low levels of trust between staff members or the culture of the school or district is not conducive to collective working, then this has to change, otherwise distributed leadership will have, at best, only an outside chance of working.

But this doesn't mean waiting forever until everything is perfect or until the school or district is completely ready. If you wait for this, you may wait indefinitely. Rather, it is about recognizing when the conditions are optimal to introduce a different way of working and when the organization is ready to engage in extended forms of distributed leadership practice.

> To what extent is leadership distributed in your organization?
>
> How effective has this been?
>
> How extended is the leadership distribution in reality?

Formal leaders in the organization are pivotally important in ensuring that distributed leadership has the best chance of working (Harris, 2013). There is just one opportunity for getting distributed leadership right. To introduce it without favorable conditions means taking the risk that it might be undermined or indeed misconstrued by others within the organization (Chapter 5). If distributed leadership is viewed as inauthentic or as simply being used as a subtle device or mechanism to manipulate others, it will be destined to fail. If so, there will be no point in trying again as those within the organization will, quite rightly, be reluctant to engage. So how does authentic distributed leadership happen in practice?

Essentially, if formal leaders create the time, space, and opportunity for colleagues to meet, plan, and reflect, it is far more likely that distributed leadership will be viewed as genuine and will be sustained. By offering staff the opportunity to lead, by inviting their participation in decision making, and by providing the time for dialogue and discussion, greater distributed leadership capacity will be created. This is not to discount, ignore, or gloss over the power dynamics in an organization or to suggest that social or cultural issues do not play out within a distributed leadership frame. They inevitably do. Rather, it is to acknowledge such tensions and challenges while simultaneously attempting to share leadership more widely and through building a more cohesive culture.

Apart from the challenges associated with the micro politics of the organization, a number of important aspects should be considered before rushing headlong into distributed leadership:

Distance: As organizations become more diverse and complex, through various partnerships and collaborations, the issue of distance makes it more difficult for professionals to meet face to face and problem solve. The physical space and distance can be a barrier to distributing leadership as the geographic separation makes it more difficult for professionals to connect and collaborate. The challenge therefore is to provide new, alternative technology-based solutions and alternative forms of communication so that professionals can lead virtually.

Culture: Distributing leadership essentially means a shift in culture away from the top-down model of leadership to a form of leadership that is more organic, spontaneous, and more difficult to control. It means a departure from a view of leadership that resides in one person to a more sophisticated and complex notion of leadership as a distributed property. The challenge therefore is to develop organizational cultures that are conducive to supporting and nurturing the interactions between individuals and teams that result in problem solving and innovation.

Structure: The way some organizations are currently organized presents a major set of barriers to distributing leadership. The structure of many schools is still dominated by compartmentalizing subjects, pupils, and learning into discrete but manageable boxes. Distributing leadership implies the erosion of these artificial barriers and implies a more fluid way of operating. The challenge therefore is to find ways of removing those structures and systems that restrict organizational learning and to replace them with mechanisms that actively support and encourage collaborative ways of working.

Inevitably, in addressing the issues of distance, structure, and culture, there will be a much greater concentration on generating great social capital (Chapter 5) through the development of skills such as building relationships, cultivating trust, growing talent, organizational redesign, and harnessing innovation. There will be an increased focus on generating and supporting collective rather than individual learning. In their work, Hargreaves and Fullan (2012, p. ix) talk about "professional capital," which they argue is the systematic integration of three kinds of capital—human, social, and decisional. Their important work reinforces the awareness that you can't get much human capital by focusing on the capital of the individual, as capital has to be circulated and shared.

> Groups, teams, and communities are far more powerful than individuals when it comes to developing human capital (Hargreaves & Fullan, 2012, p. 3).

Social capital differs from individual capital insofar as it is based on the core assumption that the group is more powerful than the individual and that collective pressure is much more likely to secure positive and long-term organizational change and improvement. In his book *Motion Leadership*, Fullan (2010b, p. 25) suggests that positive change requires a change in behaviors *before* new beliefs are established. He argues that the implication for approaching new change is pretty straightforward:

Do not load up on vision, evidence and a sense of urgency. Rather give people new experiences in relatively nonthreatening circumstances and build on it especially through interaction with trusted peers. (Fullan, 2010b, p. 25)

For those serious about distributed leadership practice, there are a number of key messages. First, give colleagues the experience of collaborating with their peers. Second, let them practice and refine their collaborative skills. And third, allow them to behave their way into authentic distributed leadership practice. Simply stating that we are going to have a model of distributed leadership in this school or district will mean very little unless a change in leaders' behaviors and beliefs follows. You can't mandate distributed leadership even though it matters. Those in formal leadership positions will need to structure opportunities so that colleagues can behave their way into a more collaborative way of working (see Chapter 8).

One thing is clear: any future leadership development has to be primarily and chiefly concerned with knowledge creation and innovation that is focused on improving learner outcomes (Harris et al., 2013). This will require continual redesign and abandoning those things that are no longer needed or simply are not fit for purpose. Under the onslaught of various initiatives, both schools and school districts are very good at "adding things"—adding yet another priority, usually generated elsewhere, on their "to do" list. Often, they are less keen and less enthusiastic at removing things or letting things go.

As new initiatives, ideas, and approaches appear or are imposed, they are somehow absorbed and integrated into the school or district, often with a great deal of dedication and hard work. High standards of professionalism mean that schools and districts want to do a great job and therefore are reluctant to remove things that they have worked hard at, simply to make room for the latest or next bright idea. As a result, many schools and districts feel the constant weight of overload and struggle on a daily basis to manage all the different responsibilities they are given.

As we are now firmly in the unchartered territory of 21st century learning, we undoubtedly need new ways of understanding, analyzing, and making sense of change. We need alternative perspectives on leadership and leadership practice. Distributed leadership offers one such perspective. It certainly isn't a panacea or blueprint for school or system transformation, but there are indications of a potentially powerful relationship between distributed forms of leadership and organizational–student outcomes. The main challenge is to develop, foster, and actively encourage new, diverse, and authentic distributed leadership forms and approaches that take schools, districts, and the entire system onward and upward. This won't be achieved by holding on to leadership structures suited, and indeed intended, for another age. It will be secured by investing in forms of future leadership that directly contribute to better organizational performance.

As the next chapter outlines, there is a growing evidence base that highlights a positive relationship between distributed leadership and organizational performance. These findings provide growing empirical support for distributed leadership as a potential influence, under the right conditions, to positively impact learning outcomes. So before getting too far into distributed leadership practice, let's consider what we know about the impact, effects, and outcomes of distributed leadership. The next chapter considers the facts.

4

Distributed Leadership: The Facts

The theories we believe we call facts and the facts we disbelieve we call theories

(Felix Cohen)

I n *Good to Great,* Jim Collins reminds us that any improvement starts with "confronting the brutal facts." In other words, look at the real issues rather than wasting time on problems that are perceived or imagined. In the increasingly commercial and lucrative world of education, it is important that school, district, and system leaders scrutinize the facts before accepting advice or adopting any changes in practice. It is important that they engage with the evidence and decide for themselves if any idea is worth pursuing or any innovation is worth implementing.

Distributed leadership, or the expansion of leadership roles, in schools, beyond those in formal leadership or administrative posts, is without question one of the most prominent ideas to emerge in the educational leadership field in recent years. Few ideas, it seems, have provoked as much enthusiasm, attention, debate, and irritation as the idea of distributed leadership! The groundbreaking work of Jim Spillane and his colleagues at Northwestern University, in the United States, sparked renewed interest in leadership *as practice* focusing particularly on the quality, nature, and type of interactions between leaders, followers, and their situation (Spillane, Halverson, & Diamond, 2001b).

While distributed leadership theory has pointed to multiple sources of influence within an organization, distributed leadership is not just a case of generating more formal roles within an organization. It is not about creating quantity but rather quality in leadership practice. The true test of distributed leadership is in the quality of the nature and interactions between individuals. As the last chapter in this book illustrates, distributed leadership can be enacted and realized through interdependent and *disciplined collaborative activity* (Harris & Jones, 2012).

A distributed model of leadership focuses upon the interactions, rather than the actions, of those in formal and informal leadership roles. It is primarily concerned with how leadership influences organizational and instructional improvement (Heck & Hallinger, 2010; Spillane, 2006). According to Spillane and Diamond (2007), distributed leadership involves two elements—the leader-plus and the practice aspect. They describe *leader-plus* as leadership when it is not attributed to formal job positions, but rather, it reflects the conjoint work of individuals toward leadership practice. The *practice aspect* reflects the interplay and the interaction of actors, artifacts, and the situation. Distributed leadership refers to both what people do (agency) and the organizational conditions in which they do it (structural aspects). Consequently, distributed leadership is a dynamic model of leadership emanating from different patterns of interaction among those in formal and informal roles.

The question of "who leads when the principal isn't leading" highlighted in an earlier chapter focuses on how those without formal leadership roles or responsibilities can be powerful instructional and curriculum leaders (Spillane, 2006).

Although a school's organizational chart may indicate a principal, assistant principal, and curriculum coordinator as the school's formal leaders, examining the school as it is lived by school staff might surface a handful of teachers or even outside professionals who serve as key leaders.

At Wayne Elementary School, located in a Chicago suburb, Karen, a newer teacher on the second-grade team, did not hold a formally designated leadership position. But the second-grade teachers, veteran and novice alike, constructed Karen as a leader for mathematics instruction by looking for her help and guidance when it came to teaching mathematics (Spillane & Coldren, 2011, p. 9).

At Silverton Elementary School, in Melbourne, Australia, the youngest and newest teacher at the school, Jane, is leading a group of more experienced colleagues in an inquiry process that is focused on improving problem-solving skills in Grade 4 students. She has no formal leadership role within the school, but every teacher in her inquiry team views her as the person who is guiding and supporting their collaborative work (Harris & Jones, 2013).

The central point here is that individuals with no designated leadership position, by virtue of the nature of their interactions with other colleagues, exercise influence related to the core business of the school; they are the leaders of instruction. Scribner, Sawyer, Watson, and Myers (2007) argue that the success of distributed leadership depends not only on individuals performing different leadership *functions* effectively but also on new patterns of *interaction and influence* among staff in the school. They see distributed leadership as social influence enacted in the cultural and behavioral interactions of people. For Karen and Jane, their ability to interact effectively with teachers who are far more experienced means that they are influencing, and they are essentially leading.

From a distributed perspective, interactions are a critical part of leadership practice. How leaders interact is considered to be more important than the exact requirements or expectations of their leadership roles, responsibilities, or functions.

While it is important to know what leaders actually do, and there is indeed a great volume of literature on this very subject, analyzing and understanding patterns of influence from a distributed perspective gets us much closer to the actual *practice* of leadership and its *impact*.

IMPACT OF DISTRIBUTED LEADERSHIP

The evidential base about the impacts and effects of distributed leadership has been summarized in numerous books and articles (Harris, 2008, 2009; Leithwood et al., 2009). Contemporary evidence increasingly points toward a positive relationship between distributed leadership, organizational improvement, and student achievement (Hallinger & Heck, 2009; Harris, 2008, 2009; Leithwood & Mascall, 2008). These studies have identified the importance of distributed leadership as a potential contributor to positive organizational change and improvement. The contemporary literature on distributed leadership also highlights that there are different patterns of leadership distribution according to

- differences in the range of organizational members to whom leadership is distributed;
- the degree to which distributed leadership forms are coordinated;
- the extent of interdependence among those to whom leadership is distributed;
- the extent to which power and authority accompany the distribution of leadership responsibilities; and
- the stimulus for leadership distribution (Day Sammons, Leithwood, Harris, & Hopkins, 2009, p. 195).

The evidence indicates that the "distribution of leadership" varies as a result of the conditions or challenges found in diverse settings. It shows, for example, that the differences between high performing and low performing schools can be attributed to different degrees of leadership distribution (Day et al., 2010; Leithwood, Harris, & Hopkins, 2008). These studies show that high performing schools have high levels of influence from all sources of leadership and that low performing schools have low levels of influence and limited leadership distribution. In another study, the leadership strategies that were linked to high performance were systematically analyzed. The findings show that clear direction from the districts and high-quality distributed leadership were central to school success.

In summary, the evidence shows that distributed leadership is an important component within and contributor to improved organizational outcomes. While there are differences in the nature, quality, and extent of distributed leadership from one context to another, it still is within the mix or amalgam of factors contributing to high performance. The research evidence also indicates that certain forms of distributed influence *have a modest but significant indirect effect on student achievement* (Leithwood & Mascall, 2008, p. 546).

So with these facts in mind, the key question is not *if* distributed leadership matters but rather *how* leadership can be distributed to matter even more.

> What are your reflections on the evidence about distributed leadership?
>
> What questions do you still have about potential benefits and limitations?

Although the evidence base on distributed school leadership highlights some of the positive effects and outcomes of leadership distribution, there is one important note of caution. Distributed leadership is not intrinsically a good or a bad thing. Like any form of leadership, it depends upon the situation and context and how it is enacted. Similarly, distributed leadership is not automatically a democratic form of leadership, as some would advocate. It is not a foregone conclusion that distributed leadership leads to a more egalitarian way of working. Much depends upon how distributed leadership is understood, deployed, and framed. Chapter 5 addresses the consequences of the different interpretation and enactment of distributed leadership.

As this chapter outlines, there are things we categorically know about distributed leadership and things we don't know. For example, we need to know much more about the patterns of distribution and understand which configurations are most likely to have a positive impact on the organization. We need to know exactly *how* distributed leadership makes a difference to organizational outcomes rather than continually seeking more confirmation that it does. We also need to be clear about the relationship between distributed leadership and organizational change.

If distributed leadership is worth taking time, effort, and resource, we had better make sure that there is something worth pursuing. Consequently, the remainder of this chapter looks at the facts. It explores the available evidence to address two key questions:

1. What evidence do we have about a positive relationship between distributed leadership and organizational improvement?

2. What are the implications for leadership development and leadership practice of a distributed approach?

But as we are dealing with facts, it is the case that distributed leadership is not an idea free of controversy or critique. Writers like Fitzgerald and Gunter (2006) and others with a similar intellectual predisposition have called into question the motivation of those espousing distributed leadership. In their view, it is possible that distributed leadership could be little more than a palatable way of encouraging teachers to do more work, a way of reinforcing standardization practices, simply "old managerialism" in a contemporary guise. Instead of being a more democratic form of leadership, they propose that distributed leadership could be another, more attractive, mechanism for delivering government policy.

While this could be construed as the case, it seems that this particular argument could be routinely applied to any new idea, initiative, or leadership approach, particularly if it does not find favor with those writing from a particular ideological position. Interestingly, in many critiques of distributed leadership, it is often difficult to see exactly what alternatives such writers are proposing. In most cases, critique is *all* that is offered, liberally sprinkled with references to Bourdieu or Foucault. So while it is accepted that there are different views on distributed leadership, some worthy of consideration, some less so, before passing judgment, let's consider exactly what the term *distributed leadership* means.

DEFINITIONS

The chameleon-like quality of the term *distributed leadership* immediately invites misinterpretation and misunderstanding (Harris, 2007). Part of the problem is that the term is "slippery" and open to many different interpretations. One common misuse of the term is that of a convenient "catch all" descriptor for any form of shared, collaborative, or extended leadership practice. This serves only to blur the meaning of distributed leadership even further. The main point here is that distributed leadership is not a form of loose cooperation or delegation by another name.

Another misconception about distributed leadership is that it is just the antithesis of top-down, hierarchical leadership. While some have positioned it in opposition to top-down models of leadership, this is a misconception and misinterpretation. Distributed leadership essentially involves *both* the vertical and lateral dimensions of leadership practice.

It encompasses *both* formal and informal forms of leadership practice within its framing, analysis, and interpretation.

> Distributed leadership embodies both *formal and informal* leadership. They are not *separate or opposite*.

Distributed leadership is primarily concerned with the *co-performance* of leadership and the *reciprocal interdependencies* that shape that leadership practice (Spillane, 2006, p. 58). This coleadership can involve both formal and informal leaders. It is not an either/or proposition as some have represented it. To position distributed leadership as the opposite of formal leadership serves only to create and maintain an unhelpful dichotomy, even if it is neatly glossed over by the idea of "hybrid leadership." It is still misleading. Also, it continues to fuel a rather redundant debate about whether hierarchical or distributed leadership might be more desirable.

The distributed perspective recognizes the possibility that people may be working together but with different goals or outcomes in mind. Work by Spillane et al. (2001b) highlights how the practice of leadership moves between those in formal and informal leadership positions. It focuses on the nature of interdependencies and the co-performance of leadership practice. Implicit in the notion of co-performance is the possibility that those performing the practice might be pursuing different or even contradictory goals. "From a distributed perspective, leaders can interact in the co-performance of leadership routines even when they seek different or conflicting outcomes" (Spillane, 2006, p. 84). This doesn't mean dissent or a breakdown in performance is inevitable.

Robinson (2008) has suggested that the nature of distributed leadership encompasses two main concepts: distributed leadership as *task distribution* and distributed leadership as distributed *influence processes*. The first has its roots in the theorization of leadership as the performance of particular tasks (Spillane, 2006), while the second emerges from the view that leadership is "an influence process that changes how others think or act with respect to the content of the influence" (Robinson, 2008, p. 246). Those in formal leadership positions therefore play a pivotal role in leadership distribution, and they are the prime influence on others and actively model reciprocal trust, responsibility, and accountability that are essential for this model of leadership to work most effectively. The research evidence underlines that without the active and full support of formal leaders in schools, then distributed leadership is unlikely to flourish or be sustained (Ban Al-Ani & Bligh, 2011; Day et al., 2009).

To varying degrees, all change flows through the principal's or superintendent's office as this is ultimately where formal responsibility lies and ultimately where the majority of final decisions are made. As Murphy, Smylie, and Seashore Louis (2009, p. 4) note, "Formal leaders are in a critical position to move initiatives forward or to kill them off, quickly through actions or slowly through neglect." In short, those with formal leadership responsibility are important gatekeepers in their schools and districts. They can actively encourage others to step up and contribute their expertise, or they can aggressively prevent others from influencing and taking the opportunity to lead (see Chapter 5.

From a distributed perspective, social interaction is a critical part of leadership practice. How leaders interact with others is viewed as more important than the precise leadership role or its leadership functions. While it is important to know what leaders actually do, and indeed there is a great amount of writing on this particular subject, case studies of their daily activity get us only so far. Analyzing and understanding patterns of influence get us much closer to understanding the actual *practice* of leadership.

> While case study accounts are interesting, they do not accurately capture the *practice* of leadership—that is, the patterns of interrelationships and complex interactions within organizations (Spillane & Coldren, 2011, p. 4).

In their study of principals in high performing schools, Day et al. (2009) highlight how the nature of the interaction and the extent of interdependence shaped the leadership task and subsequent outcomes. They note, "Leadership distribution was perceived to be an important influence on teaching and schools' change processes which affected, directly and indirectly, aspects of school culture and conditions. These indirectly impacted on improvement in pupil academic outcomes" (p. 75). This would infer that it is the practice of leadership that matters, particularly the distributed nature of that practice.

> To what extent is leadership viewed as practice in your school or district?
>
> How far does leadership equate with action rather than interactions?

Distributed leadership, as an idea, implies a fundamental change in the way formal leaders understand and view their leadership role. It also implies the relinquishing of some authority and power in order to *broker, facilitate, and support* the leadership of others (see Chapter 8). Distributed leadership also invites a very different view of the organization, one that moves away from the bureaucratic and the controlled to the integrated and the dynamic. As Murphy et al. (2009) note: "It is difficult to imagine that principals will develop the sense of security that is a necessary ingredient in the distributed leadership formula. This is challenging work, but principals that do not begin here are not likely to be effective in making distributed leadership a reality in their schools" (p. 16).

In any school, district, or system, there are inevitably many sources of influence and power, other than those emanating from the formal leadership roles. There will be those with personal power, by virtue of personality, experience, or the support of peers, who may not be in any formal role but who can greatly influence others for good or ill (Chapter 5). But where there is purposeful, planned, and aligned distributed leadership, rather than random, ill-disciplined, or chaotic distributed leadership practice, the difference in organizational outcomes can be quite dramatic. So what does the evidence show about the impact of planned and aligned distributed leadership? What, if anything, does it say, with certainty, about its positive influence and effects?

Distributed Leadership: What We Know

Later in the chapter, the evidential base will be outlined in more detail, but at the outset just to summarize, here are the things that we know. First, we know that there are beneficial effects, to the organization, of wider leadership distribution. Second, distributed leadership can have a positive effect on teaching and learning outcomes (Camburn & Han 2009; Hallinger & Heck, 2009; Leithwood et al., 2009). Third, the configuration of leadership distribution is important, and certain patterns of distribution have a more positive effect than others upon organizational development and change (Leithwood et al., 2007, 2009). This takes us to the fourth clear finding from the research evidence, concerning successful and high performing organizations. The evidence shows such organizations tend to have extended forms of distributed leadership practice (Hargreaves et al., 2010).

So what about distributed leadership and learner outcomes? Without question, this is the most controversial and contested area among those writing and researching in this area. Positions on the relationship between distributed leadership and student learning outcomes vary. Some writers have argued that seeking to explore this relationship is a futile exercise. Others have argued that distributing leadership is desirable only if the quality of leadership activities contributes to "assisting teachers to provide more effective instruction to their students" (Timperley, 2007). But what does the evidence actually show?

There are a limited number of studies that have explicitly explored the relationship between distributed leadership and learner outcomes. However, three studies, in particular, offer a useful starting point in highlighting what we know about distributed leadership and student learning outcomes. The first study suggests that distributing a larger proportion of leadership activity to teachers has a positive influence on teacher effectiveness and student engagement (Leithwood & Jantzi, 2000). The study analysts also note that teacher leadership has a significant effect on student engagement that far outweighs principal leadership effects after taking into account home family background.

A second study also provides confirmation of the key processes through which more distributed kinds of leadership influence student learning outcomes (Silins & Mulford, 2002). This work concluded that student outcomes are more likely to improve when leadership sources are distributed throughout the school community and when teachers are empowered in areas of importance to them. A third study conducted in England found positive relationships between the degree of teachers' involvement in decision making and student motivation and self-efficacy (Harris & Muijs, 2004). This study explored the relationship between teacher involvement in decision making within the school and a range of student outcomes. The findings reveal a positive relationship between distributed leadership and student engagement. In addition, both teacher and student morale improve where teachers feel more included and involved in decision making within the school.

Other contemporary work that has focused upon distributed leadership and instructional change includes work by Camburn and Han (2009), who explored the outcomes of distributed leadership by drawing upon extensive evidence from an investigation into the America's Choice Comprehensive School Reform program. This study concluded that distributing leadership to teachers can support positive instructional change. In their research, Hallinger and Heck (2009) explored the impact of system policies on the development of distributed school leadership and school improvement. Their quantitative analysis and results support a relationship between distributed leadership and school capacity for improvement. They conclude that distributed leadership is an important co-effect of school improvement processes.

Similarly, research by Day et al. (2009, p. 17) showed that substantial leadership distribution was very important to a school's success in *improving pupil outcomes*. The findings from this study showed that distributed leadership was positively correlated to the conditions within the organization, including staff morale, which in turn impacted positively upon student behavior and student learning outcomes.

In summary, the empirical evidence about the relationship between distributed leadership and student outcomes is encouraging. It shows that distributed leadership if properly planned and enacted has the potential to be a positive influence on organizational change and improvement. Possibly for this reason alone, distributed leadership is part of the educational policy makeup in many different countries around the world.

Distributed leadership is increasingly being viewed, at school, district, and system levels, as a strategic lever for building the collective capacity for change. Countries such as England, Malaysia, Australia, Wales, and parts of Europe are including distributed leadership as part of their system reform process (Wheldon, 2009). In England, distributed leadership underpins the new models of schooling, in particular the collaborative working of chains of academies and federations of schools (Chapman et al., 2010). In many Scandinavian countries, distributed leadership is concomitant with the principles and practice of democratic education (Moos, 2007). In the Netherlands, a leadership competency framework has been developed that reflects the principles of distributed leadership (Kruger, 2009), and in Norway, successful headship is associated with distributed leadership practice (Moller et al., 2005).

In Wales, distributed leadership is a key part of system-wide reform and manifests itself most clearly in the national program of professional learning communities (Harris, 2013;

Harris & Jones, 2010). In Australia, the national government has invested in a new organization[1] that is supporting and developing collaborative leadership practices as a contributor to professional learning. In Malaysia, distributed leadership is part of the "blueprint" for system reform (Ministry of Education [MOE], 2012), and in Singapore, Hong Kong, and Shanghai, professional collaboration is a hallmark of high performance and a key reason for their continued success (Harris et al., 2013; Jensen, 2012).

But despite a groundswell of enthusiasm for distributed leadership, there are some limitations, some barriers, and some challenges. In the pursuit of better outcomes for all young people whatever the country, there are always difficult decisions to make and potential trade-offs to be considered. As highlighted earlier, distributed leadership does not guarantee better performance; it is not a magic bullet for success. So much depends on how leadership is distributed and the intentions behind the distribution. As Spillane and Coldren (2011, p. 109) note at the end of their book,

> While some readers may be looking for a quick fix to improve teaching and learning in their schools, we have intentionally tried to avoid offering prescriptive recipes for school leadership and management that school leaders are meant to implement intact. Because schools and their leaders are situated in time and place, it would be imprudent for us to outline a list of steps for leaders to follow with the promise of a pot of gold at the end of the school improvement rainbow. While schools share many commonalities, every school also has some unique situations, with an organizational infrastructure comprised of the potential for a variety of formal positions and organizational routines, a staff with students, families, community and district and state level stakeholders. (p. 109)

---

[1] Australian Institute for Teaching and School Leadership.

The point these authors are making is a valid one. Schools vary considerably, from one another even in the same district, city, town, or village. Therefore, the one-size-fits-all approach to school improvement is not something that is worth pursuing as ultimately, like a one-size-fits-all T-shirt, it fits no one. However, I tend to disagree that the differences within and between schools are so great that we cannot arrive at some common denominator factors for change and improvement, that if properly contextualized could be helpful or useful to schools or districts. While it is right to avoid naive improvement prescriptions or checklists predicated on uniformity, it is also important to acknowledge that there are enough similarities between schools and districts to make the deployment of certain strategies and approaches worthwhile, whatever the differences in context.

The evidence contained in this chapter suggests that distributed leadership is an idea worth consideration, if organizational change and improvement is the end game. Subsequent chapters (6, 7, and 8) therefore look at the implications, practicalities, and conditions for making distributed leadership happen. But before moving too quickly into application, there is an important note of caution. As highlighted earlier, no assumption is being made here that distributed leadership is inherently a good or a bad thing. It is not "friend or foe" (Harris, 2013), but as with any form of power, authority, or influence, it can be used or misused.

Consequently, the next chapter looks at the more negative aspects of distributed leadership, or the "dark side." This is not to be overly pessimistic or to cast a shadow over the more fruitful aspects of this form of leadership. Rather, the intention is to be realistic and to offer a balanced argument in this book through exploring both the potential and the pitfalls of a distributed leadership approach. Distributed leadership, like any other form of leadership, is directly concerned with the complex interplay and dynamics of power and authority. The next chapter looks at the consequences for individuals and organizations when such power and authority is misused.

5

Distributed Leadership: The Dark Side

Collaborative cultures, which by definition have close relationships, are indeed powerful, but unless they focus on the right things they may end up being powerfully wrong

(Fullan, 2012)

Think about a leader, right now. I guarantee that an image will pop into your head of Gandhi, Mandela, or Mother Teresa. We tend to think of leaders as inherently good. The leadership literature is full of individual accounts of triumph, heroism, stories of overcoming the odds, and reflections on exceptional careers. The "I did it my way" leadership literature still dominates and prevails because essentially we like heroes and we desperately want to believe in them. The bulk of the leadership literature and indeed most of the writing on educational leadership mostly reinforces that leadership is a powerful force for good. Usually this is the case but not always.

In *The Dark Side of Educational Leadership: Superintendents and the Professional Victim Syndrome*, the authors provide valuable insights into the ways in which leaders can create professional victims (Poka & Litchka, 2008). They argue that leadership can be a very negative influence that can cause individuals severe pain and damage. Most specifically, they illuminate the factors that contribute most often to the victimization of superintendents and the undermining of professional confidence and expertise. They highlight the potential for bullying those in positions of power and illuminate how leadership can be a negative force when in the wrong hands.

Conversely, most of the academic research and writing about leadership focuses on the positive attributes and characteristics of leadership. It tends to emphasize a wholesome relationship between leaders and their followers. For many years, social scientists have emphasized the positive attributes of leadership and the positive intentions behind leadership practices. There is, however, a line of research that is much less developed. This work has focused upon the negative aspects of leadership actions and behaviors including the destructive aspects of leadership, such as aggressive, bullying, and undermining leadership practices (Blase & Blase, 2003).

The reasons for these negative leadership behaviors seem to vary considerably from being an aspect of personality, a function of the nature of the responses from followers, or the cultural context that these leaders find themselves located within. For example, destructive leaders may come with a whole set of negative personality characteristics that manifest themselves mostly in the workplace where they have positional power and authority. It may be that the passive nature of the followers or their unwillingness to respond to the leader's requests can fuel a leader's bad behavior. Or it could simply be that the leader is located in an environment where the pressure and stress to perform is such that this is reflected in the way that he or she leads. Potentially and explosively, it could be a function of all three.

Whatever the origin, source, or driver of destructive leadership, it is much more prevalent than the literature actually acknowledges or admits. Harmful leadership is substantially more damaging to individuals than is realized or accepted. Part of the reason why the issue of "bad" leadership remains under the radar is the reluctance among those who experience this form of institutional and personal bullying to speak about it. Everyone wants to talk about a great leader, to share their stories of charismatic leadership, to pile on the praise—but who wants to admit to being intimidated, bullied, or made to feel worthless by their boss.

Have you ever experienced "a bad leader"?

How did that affect you, your work?

In your experience, are there any ways to manage a bad leader?

The prime reason for raising this issue of negative or bad leadership is to reflect upon what happens when distributed leadership is used or abused. What happens when a leader is trying to control rather than empower? Conversely, what happens to the formal leaders when those who are authentically and genuinely invited to take more power and authority subsequently abuse it?

This chapter looks at the dark side of distributed leadership. It looks at what happens when distributed leadership is used as a subtle form of manipulation and control. As noted in the preface, some writers have called into question the motivation of those espousing distributed leadership, particularly in a normative way. In their view, distributed leadership is little more than a palatable way of encouraging teachers to do more work, a way of reinforcing standardization practices in a contemporary guise. Instead of being a more democratic form of leadership, Hargreaves and Fink (2009) warn that distributed leadership could simply be another, more attractive, mechanism for delivering top-down policies. In addition, other critics point to the ways in which distributed leadership could be willfully misunderstood or misrepresented (Bolden, Petrov, & Gosling, 2009).

The way people understand the term *distributed leadership* and relay the concept to others is important. Discussions about distributed leadership will inevitably end prematurely if it is perceived by those within the organization to simply be the allocation of more work. If distributed leadership is viewed as adding to the daily workload, then resistance is to be anticipated. Whatever the words used by school leaders or superintendents to explain, describe, or promote distributed leadership, those on the receiving end may have a completely different conception and interpretation of what is being asked of them. Thus, it is important to be clear about intentions and expectations as, when not adequately explained, distributed leadership can be easily misconstrued as delegation or even subtle coercion (Hatcher, 2005).

Any misunderstanding of the term *distributed leadership* will result in unintended outcomes. So, for example, if a principal or superintendent talks the language of empowerment or collective engagement but in reality allocates unwanted tasks to others, then his or her version of distributed leadership will soon be viewed as inauthentic and disingenuous. If there is a mismatch between the sound track (i.e., what is spoken) and the action (i.e., what happens in practice)—any initial buy-in will soon be lost (Hatcher, 2005). Formal leaders are the gatekeepers of change, and they can be a help or a hindrance in securing new ways of working.

DISTRIBUTED LEADERSHIP: LEADING OR MISLEADING?

In the case of distributed leadership, those in formal leadership positions can actually be an impediment for a number of key reasons. First, some formal leaders see distributed leadership as the relinquishing of power and control as if they have *lost* some authority or influence. So often, I hear the comment, "If I give others the opportunity to lead, that means that I am less powerful." Interestingly, the most effective leaders know that empowering others is the act of a strong leader and not a weak one. The examples of leadership in high performance organizations showed again and again that the leaders were ambitious for their organization and not themselves. They readily and carefully distributed leadership because it made their organization stronger and more competitive (Hargreaves et al., 2010).

A second impediment to distributed leadership occurs when those in formal power choose or involve only those who support their particular agenda. This selective distributed leadership is inauthentic, and ultimately, any benefit from this form of distributed leadership will be short-lived. Third, if formal leaders distribute leadership but continually double check on those with newfound authority, then this approach is also unlikely to work. In short, any inauthentic attempts at distributed leadership, whatever form they take, ultimately will prove to be counterproductive (Hatcher, 2005).

In her synthesis of the limitations of distributed leadership, Wright (2008) adds to the list of potential impediments. She argues that a distributed framework "gives minimal attention to the roles, responsibilities or circumstances under which the formal leader (i.e. the principal or superintendent) *must* exercise leadership. To simply ignore the legislation and policies that define the role of the principal, and hold principals accountable for their actions and school-based results, would pose significant ethical, professional and organizational concerns" (p. 3). The implication here is that those writing about distributed leadership have somehow discounted the requirements of the formal leadership role.

Without question, the formal responsibilities of the principal or superintendent cannot be overlooked or ignored. This is certainly not the position taken or, indeed, advocated by those writing about distributed leadership in this book or any other. The contracted duties and responsibilities of those in formal leadership roles should not be, and indeed cannot be, ignored or reallocated. But surely leadership is much more than just the core duties and associated responsibilities of the role? These contractual responsibilities matter, of course, but the best leaders go way beyond the terms and conditions of their contract. They deliver more than the bare minimum that their duties define and outline. The best leaders actively seek opportunities to develop, grow, and change their organization for the better.

A contemporary study of high performing organizations found several common attributes of the leaders who excelled (Hargreaves et al., 2010). First, these exceptional leaders could fulfill the routine and contractual parts of their jobs in their sleep; these responsibilities were certainly not the main source of their success. Second, these high performing leaders actively sought out new challenges; they aggressively sought out new opportunities and thrived on taking new risks. Complacency was not a word in their vocabulary; they excelled when their organization was on the move and doing things differently from the competition.

Interestingly, at one time, each of the high performing leaders in the Performance Beyond Expectations study had faced abject failure. For Stuart Rose, CEO of the retail giant Marks and Spencer, it was the prospect of losing its top place in retailing and being taken over by another major company. For Cricket Australia, it was the humiliation of losing the Ashes to England. In Central School in Gloucester, in the South of England, it was the prospect of facing closure because of low results. For ShoeBuy.com in Boston, in the United States, it was the dot–com meltdown. While failure in the sporting, business, or, indeed, educational world is not uncommon, the response to failure is what defines outstanding and exceptional leaders.

To summarize, each of the high performing leaders chose to resolve a situation that, on the face of it, looked hopeless. None of these leaders checked their job description before taking on the challenge; they simply did what was required of them to ensure that their organization survived and, subsequently, thrived. While roles and responsibilities have to be fulfilled, a central part of the job of any formal leader is also to develop the organization and provide opportunities for those within it to lead and to learn. As the research has categorically shown, the formal leader's influence and actions largely determine whether an organization succeeds or fails (Leithwood, Harris, & Hopkins, 2008). It is also clear that the very best leaders put people before terms and conditions. Creating organizations where relationships matter and where everyone's contribution is valued is what characterizes effective leadership (see Chapter 6). The most effective leaders understand that people are not just their *best asset*, as Microsoft would argue. They are their *only* asset.

Leading is essentially a social process, and where human beings are involved, there are no surefire certainties. There will be those in formal leadership roles who espouse the virtues of distributed leadership, while surreptitiously using it to manipulate, control, and coerce those without power, authority, or voice. There will be those who advocate collaborative working, while undermining any attempt at genuine collective working. There is no watertight assurance that distributed leadership or any other form of leadership will have a positive impact; as highlighted earlier, it is not friend or foe. As Scribner, Sawyer, Watson, and Myers (2007) note:

> Distributed leadership can just as easily be associated with the negative qualities of organizations as it can be with the positive. Oppressive and controlling structures can take form in a context of collaboration and apparent shared governance. They are not limited to traditional hierarchical models of organizations. Collaboration does not necessarily equate with workers becoming more creative and innovative. In fact the opposite can occur. (p. 94)

Some leaders may genuinely believe that they are authentically distributing leadership, but the feedback from others may suggest that this is simply not the case (Department for Education and Skills, 2007). Rather than distributed leadership, there is "distributed pain" where distributed leadership equates with work intensification (Youngs, 2009, p. 7). Distributing pain, however, is not restricted only to those on the receiving end of top-down leadership practices.

Those formal leaders supporting and encouraging distributed leadership, within their organization, can also find that out the hard way that when it is deliberately misused, distributed leadership can be a potentially damaging force. This darker side of distributed leadership can be best illustrated through real experience.

Over the years, many school and district leaders have shared the darker side of distributed leadership with me personally. They have highlighted how, if misused or misapplied, distributed leadership can disempower, disrupt, and even derail those in formal leadership roles. If too much power, authority, and influence are absorbed and taken by those who have the opportunity to misuse and abuse them, the net result can be disastrous. All their examples tell a similar story:

Superintendent X runs a very effective district and has generated a high degree of trust among staff. The superintendent is well respected and liked. The district has embraced distributed leadership through extensive teamwork, and people are actively encouraged to take responsibility and to lead. At first, the superintendent maintains a good balance of power between the formal and informal leadership. Over time, however, the workload of the superintendent intensifies, and a few employees contrive to use their new influence and authority to deliberately undermine the formal leadership.

The superintendent and others in formal leadership roles are totally unaware of this negative pattern of behavior, as it remains subtle and covert. The few employees use their new influence to create unrest and to actively seek to undermine those in formal leadership positions. Over time, the power base shifts and conflict gradually erodes collaboration.

In time, there is a concerted effort by the subversives to remove those in the formal leadership roles in order to move into this space or to simply disrupt the status quo. The superintendent is faced with the choice of leaving the district or trying to reassert authority and to regain control in the face of strong opposition. The balance of power has shifted, and the pattern of leadership distribution is no longer one that supports organizational improvement.

Fortunately, examples like this are not common and are certainly not the norm, but they happen. So what are the lessons?

First, this example raises an issue about the nature and degree of influence that others have within the organization. Maintaining a balance is critically important. Whatever the pattern of distribution, it will be essential that the formal leaders set the boundaries plus the overall direction and do not relinquish control over final decision making. Second, those in formal leadership positions will need to ensure that effective monitoring and feedback systems are in place so any issues or problems come to the surface quickly, so they can be dealt with openly and transparently.

Third, distributed leadership means that different leaders at different times will emerge because of their particular experience and expertise. The main lesson is to keep distributed leadership fluid and moving so no one individual or group secures a power base or attempts to misuse their newfound influence for negative purposes. Finally, within the organization, it needs to be clear that the informal leadership is not fixed or permanent and can be recalibrated at any time.

Have you ever found yourself in a position where your authority or power was deliberately undermined? How did this turn out?

How could you safeguard this from happening within a context of widely distributed leadership?

It takes a secure and strong leader to be able to facilitate distributed leadership while also retaining a firm hold on the overall direction of the organization. It takes a leader who can empower but can also intervene, if the extended leadership activity is misaligned or having a negative impact upon the organization. It also requires a leader who understands and can overcome some of the inherent barriers to distributed leadership practice.

BARRIERS TO DISTRIBUTED LEADERSHIP

Apart from the willful misuse of distributed leadership for personal gain, there are other barriers that can easily derail and undermine this leadership approach. As noted earlier, by confronting the brutal facts, more opportunity exists to reduce and ameliorate the potential impact of certain barriers. From working with many schools and districts in various countries, there have been many opportunities to ask practitioners about the potential barriers to distributed leadership. Without fail, there is normally an enthusiastic response when groups are asked about the barriers to distributed leadership. It seems that problems are always easier to identify than solutions.

From the helpful feedback from various groups of practitioners, certain barriers to distributed leadership have been consistently identified. The following list is therefore illustrative rather than definitive.

Time. Somewhat predictably time always appears at the top of the list. Where do busy teachers and district staff find the time to lead innovation and change? Why should they devote time away from their core work? On most days, teachers and district staff rarely have the opportunity to have a coffee break let alone take on leadership responsibility, so how is distributed leadership feasible?

Clearly, there are no easy or magic answers to producing more time. However, in addressing this question, it is important to ask whether there is anything more important than developing others or anything more pressing than organizational improvement? Furthermore, in most schools and districts, a great deal of time is devoted to routine and unproductive meetings. A savvy principal or superintendent can find time for colleagues to engage in leading innovation by rearranging formal meetings or by using professional learning time more effectively. The real issue is not about finding *extra time* but in using the existing time *more productively.* Clearly, much depends on the core priorities of the school or the district. If professional learning and collaborative inquiry are considered centrally important because they directly impact upon learning (student and professional), then this may be the core priority. This is where time should be spent.

Culture. In some schools or districts, the culture itself can prove a barrier to distributed leadership. The key conditions (e.g., trust, respect, mutual learning) may not be in place to fully support it. As noted earlier, under certain circumstances, organizations will find it more or less possible to distribute leadership.

The culture is an important factor, but it is also important to recognize that the way leadership is shared and distributed can, in itself, have a powerful impact on cultural norms, the "ways of working around here." So if the culture isn't right for distributed leadership, it possibly isn't ideal for innovation and change either. It will be important therefore to generate some structural change within the organization to start to disrupt and alter the current ways of working and to instigate some changes that will require greater teamwork and collaborative practices.

Professional Reluctance. Resistance to working in this way is obviously a big barrier to distributed leadership. What if others don't see themselves as leaders? What if they do not want to lead? What if it is not in their job description and there is no remuneration for the additional work? This is a reasonable position to take when professionals are faced with more responsibility or anticipating that much more work will be placed squarely on their shoulders.

This is where the culture of the school or district matters a great deal. Within the organization, if there is a clear demarcation between roles and responsibilities and "no remuneration, no participation" is the mantra of the staff, then those interested in distributed leadership will face an uphill struggle. Possibly, one way forward is to remind teachers or district personnel that they lead in the classroom and the district, every day, and that it is only through sharing their expertise that any improvement is either realistic or sustainable.

It is also the case that for most professionals, their own professional development is seen as a core entitlement. While this is usually translated as a course or workshop, as argued in a later chapter, the most effective form of professional learning occurs in collaborative teams. By underlining that distributed leadership is chiefly about giving those with the experience, knowledge, and skill the opportunity to lead, it might encourage those who are reluctant to think again.

However, if there is tenacious resistance from certain staff members, it is important for formal leaders to devote their time and energy to those staff who are more enthusiastic, more engaged, and more energized. Often, leaders can spend a disproportionate amount of time on people who will never ever move to action. There is a saying, "don't water the rocks." In short, ensure that you are not just wasting your valuable time and energy on the people who will never change—look to the others who are keen to be involved.

Getting It Wrong. A significant barrier to distributed leadership is the fear of making errors or mistakes. For those in formal leadership roles, it is the potential for things to go in a different direction or to go off track that is of most concern. The higher probability of this happening equates with the feeling of relinquishing control. Similarly, for those who are now leading innovation and change, the pressure of getting it wrong can also be quite daunting.

The whole point of distributed leadership is creativity and not conformity: to try new things and to test them out, to make mistakes so that learning takes place. It is pointless investing time and energy in revisiting safe but ultimately tired old ideas.

Are there any other barriers to distributed leadership that you have identified?

In what ways might they be overcome?

For formal leaders who are facilitating and supporting distributed leadership, there has to be an adherence to "no blame" innovation. So if things go "wrong" it will be important for those with ultimate responsibility to remind people that making mistakes is acceptable and, in fact, is a very important part of learning. Unintended outcomes are sometimes more important than those that are foreseen or planned. Similarly, for those leading innovation, it will be important that the changes generated or proposed are within the organization's overall priorities.

For many schools and districts, the idea of distributed leadership itself can prove to be a significant challenge: it requires a reevaluation of what leadership means, how it is enacted, and most importantly who leads. It is naive to believe that distributed leadership is a straightforward or easy proposition. This is certainly not what this book is attempting to advocate or argue. Indeed, the converse is true.

Making distributed leadership happen is fundamentally about recognizing that within any organization there is expertise and influence that is untapped and that could be better utilized, if only the opportunities were provided. It is the job of the school or district leader to create these opportunities. As we have seen, without the support of the formal leader, distributed leadership cannot take place in an authentic way. The very best leaders ensure that every last drop of expertise is devoted to improving organizational performance and outcomes (Hargreaves et al., 2010). They build collective capacity and maximize *social capital* as a way of securing productive change.

The next chapter takes a more detailed look at the idea of social capital and explores the links between social capital and distributed leadership. This chapter sets the foundation for Chapters 7 and 8 by arguing that organizational change and improvement requires collective capacity building.

6

Distributed Leadership: Building Social Capital

A basic tenet of almost all social capital theories is that a network is one of the most powerful assets that any individual can possess. It provides access to power, information, knowledge

(Prusak & Cohen, 2001)

One of the deepest human desires is to be understood. But real understanding can be achieved only through connecting and interacting with others. It is through social connections that the best and most effective learning takes place. This is also the case for professional learning. When the vast amount of writing about professional learning is analyzed, it is clear that when professionals collaborate on real issues, problems, or challenges that fundamentally matter to them, then the potential for mutual learning can be quite dramatic. The important point here is that the quality of an individual's professional learning depends on the quality of collective learning and vice versa. In short, learning collaboratively depends on trust and authentic interdependence. It depends on generating *social* rather than *individual* capital.

This chapter considers the relationship between distributed leadership practice and social capital. This chapter aims to address two questions: First, how can we build and sustain social capital? Second, how can distributed or collaborative leadership contribute to building social capital for organizational improvement? But what is social capital exactly, and why does it matter?

The World Bank defines social capital as the "norms and social relationships embedded in structures that enable people to co-ordinate action to achieve desired goals" (World Bank, 1999). In their work, Cohen and Prusak (2001) define social capital as the "stock of active connections between people, the trust, mutual understanding and shared values and behaviours that bind the members of human networks and communities together and make co-operative action possible" (p. 4). The essence of *social capital* therefore is equitable participation in a joint enterprise, implying shared or distributed leadership and interdependent or collaborative working.

The central argument throughout this chapter is that distributed leadership, in the form of professional or disciplined collaboration,[1] can build social capital, which in turn can contribute to organizational performance and outcomes. Social capital is important because it has the potential to make a difference to organizational performance and improvement. The diagram on the next page summarizes this interrelationship.

---

[1]Note the definition of *disciplined collaboration* outlined by Harris and Jones (2012).

Improving Organizational Performance and Outcomes

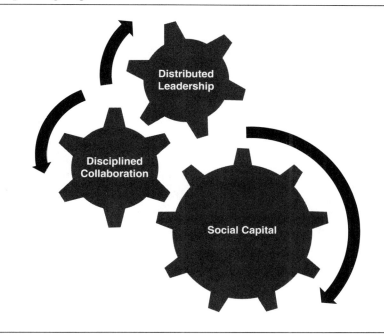

Within the business world, and to varying degrees within educational policy making, there is still a preoccupation with individual performance, accountability, and competition as the main drivers of change, improvement, and performance. Despite the fact that the return on the investment of such approaches has not been uniformly proven, this rational, instrumental, and essentially "human capital" approach still prevails in the pursuit of boardroom and classroom improvement. As Hargreaves and Shirley (2012) point out, "Accountability is the remainder that is left when responsibility has been subtracted" (p. 62). They argue that *collective professional responsibility* precedes and supersedes accountability, citing the example of "high performing" Finland, where there is no word for accountability and where "the teaching force can be trusted to produce quality learning in each and every locality" (p. 63). Success is dependent upon much more than simply individual performance or human capital.

Recent research has shown that while investing in human capital is an important factor in securing better organizational performance, significantly greater benefits can be obtained from generating collective or social capital. In her work, Leana (2011) reminds us,

> Social capital is not a characteristic of the individual teacher but instead resides in the relationships among teachers. In response to the question "Why are some teachers better than others?" a human capital perspective would answer that some teachers are just better trained, more gifted, or more motivated. A social capital perspective would answer the same question by looking not just at what a teacher knows, but also where she gets that knowledge. If she has a problem with a particular student, where does the teacher go for information and advice? Who does she use to sound out her own ideas or assumptions about teaching? Who does she confide in about the gaps in her understanding of her subject knowledge? (p. 3)

Social capital is essentially concerned with the norms and networks that support and facilitate collective actions for *mutual* benefit (Preece, 2002). Social capital exists and resides in the relationships and interactions of individuals rather than in the characteristics or skill sets of the individuals themselves. These relationships form the complex web of interactions and communications which is a powerful catalyst for collective improvement.

Social capital can be summarized into the simple but powerful idea that "relationships matter." But it is not just about building positive relationships—it is what those relationships actually *achieve* that matters most of all. We have all been in the position where relationships are socially good but productivity is really low. Sometimes, productivity is sacrificed in order to keep the friendships or relationships that matter much more to individuals. So while relationship building is important, relationship building with purpose is far more likely to secure productive and positive change.

Evidence suggests that by focusing upon and by improving productive relationships, leaders can alter an entire organization's capacity to learn, for the better (West-Burnham & Otero, 2004, p. 4). Signaling that relationships matter in achieving better outcomes can significantly affect the culture of the organization. It reinforces the idea that people come first and are central to future improvement, if they work productively together. This, in turn, can shift attitudes and can change behaviors in ways that are more conducive to higher performance.

In *Great by Choice: Uncertainty, Chaos and Luck—Why Some Thrive Despite Them All,* Jim Collins and Morten Hansen (2011) talk about seven companies that have survived and, indeed, thrived in changing and challenging circumstances over a fifteen-year period. These "10X companies" have outperformed competitors by more than ten-fold on their respective industry indexes. In this book, Collins and Hansen conclude that innovation alone is not the secret of lasting success but that the 10X companies had the ability to blend creativity with discipline to achieve their desired outcomes. They also established strong, cohesive cultures where engagement, mutual understanding, and productivity were critical to achieving better outcomes.

In *Great by Choice,* collaboration has been shown to be a vital skill that teams and companies utilize in order to constantly create, innovate, and adapt to change. This skill is not only the preserve of corporations and businesses-as their example of Alice Byrne Elementary School, in Yuma, Arizona, reveals:

In 1997, Alice Byrne Elementary School, in Yuma, Arizona, performed no better than a similar comparison school and substantially below

(Continued)

(Continued)

state averages in third-grade reading. Principal Julie Tate Peach refused to capitulate to difficult circumstances. Yes, many of the kids came from poor Latino families. Yes, the school had a limited budget. Yes, the teachers felt stretched to do more with less. Peach and her teachers nonetheless overcame these obstacles and gradually increased student reading performance by about 20 percentage points to beat state averages. Meanwhile Alice Byrne's comparison school, facing similar circumstances, demonstrated no substantial improvement in third-grade reading. Why?

Julie Tate Peach created a collaborative culture of teachers and administrators poring over data and sharing ideas for how to help each child perform better. They embraced a never-ending cycle of instruction, assessment, and intervention, kid by kid. . . . Improving results increased confidence and motivation, which then reinforced discipline, which then drove up results, which increased confidence and motivation, which reinforced discipline, up and up and up.

Source: Collins and Hansen (2011, p. 57).

The authors highlight that the school "beat the odds," not by grasping for the next fad or fashion but from working together in a focused and systematic way to secure better outcomes and higher achievement. They also talk about collaborating in a "disciplined" way. Collins and Hansen (2011), however, outline a very *different* interpretation of disciplined collaboration than that outlined in the last chapter of this book.

Essentially, in their seven business settings, disciplined collaboration is described as "a creative planning and a decision-making process" (Collins & Hansen, 2011, p. 35). In contrast, the idea of disciplined collaboration used in this book and others (Jones, 2013) encompasses much more than planning and decision making. Here, disciplined collaboration is associated with a clear collaborative methodology that is consistently and rigorously applied so that there is a *positive impact* (Harris & Jones, 2012). The main point of disciplined collaboration is "to connect to learn" so that better outcomes follow for learners, professionals, and the organization (Chapter 8).

Conversely, in *Great by Choice,* disciplined collaboration is defined and characterized as "consistency of action." Undoubtedly, consistency is important in securing meaningful change, but so much depends on whether it is the *right* action in the first place. If not, all that happens is that the teams or groups consistently get it *wrong.* While it may be true that two heads are better than one—if the two heads think the same, then collaboration will yield relatively little. As Chapter 8 outlines, disciplined professional collaboration means that low-level consensus is not an option however consistently that might be achieved.

But more about the practicalities of securing effective professional collaborative comes up a little later on. Let's return to social capital and the important issue of generating trust and building collective capacity.

TRUST AND COLLECTIVE CAPACITY BUILDING

Without exception, the core role of the principals or superintendents is first and foremost to build relational trust. In their seminal work on the importance of social trust in schools, Bryk and Schneider (2002) identify four aspects of relational trust that directly contribute to building social capital. These are as follows:

1. Respect—do we acknowledge one another's dignity and ideas?

2. Competence—do we believe in each other's ability to fulfill our responsibilities?

3. Personal regard—do we care about each other enough to go the extra mile?

4. Integrity—do we trust each other to put children's needs first even in the face of tough decisions?

> How would your organization rate using these four criteria? How high is the level of trust where you work?

In the businesss world, the importance of authentic trust in securing better outcomes and performance is widely known. In *The Speed of Trust: The One Thing that Changes Everything,* by Stephen M. R. Covey with Rebecca R. Merrill, the authors clearly show, through many examples, how the *trust = organizational improvement* relationship works in practice. In their book, they convincingly argue that the quality of an organization, that is, its efficiency and its effectiveness, comes down to one thing and one thing only: how far and how quickly you *trust others* within the organization. The faster the transfer of trust, or its speed, the better the potential for organizational improvement and higher performance.

While effective organizations have positive relationships and open, trusting cultures, in direct contrast, ineffective organizations are characterized by dysfunctional relationships and low levels of trust. They are cultures where dialogue is absent, but gossip is rife, where the adults do not enage in a positive way, if indeed at all, and there is constant low-level squabbling and continual turf wars. Changing such cultures or improving dysfunctional organizations will require a radical change in the social dynamics and a significant shift in the quality of relationships. It will require modeling by the leaders about the type of relationships that are acceptable and how to positively interact with others.

In summary, the main differences between the characteristics of high performing and low performing organizations can be delineated as follows.

High Performance	Low Performance
Relational Trust	Suspicion and Mistrust
Open Communication	Covert Communication

(Continued)

High Performance	Low Performance
Transparency and Openness	Secrecy and Closed Attitudes
Distributed, Collaborative Leadership	Autocratic, Dictatorial Leadership
Collective Working	Individual Working
Interdependent Learning	Dependent Learning
Constant Reinvention	Conformity
Innovation	Repetition
New Ideas Generated	Existing Ideas Recycled
Future Oriented	Preoccupied With the Past
Collective Capacity Building	Complacency

Organizations that reflect the right-hand column are stuck. The internal dynamics are such that any intervention or innovation is unlikely to succeed because the conditions are simply not favorable and the culture is predisposed to reject rather than accept new ideas. So let's imagine you work in an organization just like this; could it be moved or changed for the better, and if so how?

The short answer is yes. There is a great deal of research showing that failing schools, failing businesses, and even failing school systems can turnaround and improve (Leithwood, Strauss, & Harris, 2010). Considering exactly how to make turnaround a reality, however, places us in much more complex territory without any silver bullets or magic remedies. But two things we know. First, successful turnaround requires capacity building to make it happen at all, and second, it requires collective capacity building to make it happen quickly.

COLLECTIVE CAPACITY BUILDING

Let's look at the idea of *collective capacity building* in a little more detail as it is here that ideas about distributed leadership, collaboration, and social capital collide and coalesce. Within any organization, there is capacity at different levels: for individuals, *personal capacity;* in groups, through *collective capacity;* and in whole organizations, whether schools, districts, or governments, through *organizational capacity.* Lieberman (1995, p. 5) suggests that educational reform depends on teachers' individual and collective capacity and notes that it is only through development of individuals that collective capacity can be secured.

Essentially, capacity building means that people take the opportunity to do things differently, to learn new skills, and to generate more effective practice. Fullan (2010a, p. 57) has suggested that collective "capacity building concerns competencies, resources and motivation. Individuals and groups are high in capacity if they possess and continue to develop the knowledge and skills if they are committed to putting the energy to get important things done collectively and continuously." As Fullan notes:

> The power of collective capacity is that it enables ordinary people to accomplish extraordinary things—for two reasons. One is that knowledge about effective practice becomes more widely available and accessible on a daily basis. The second reason is more powerful still—working together generates commitment. Moral purpose, when it stares you in the face through students and your peers working together to make lives and society better, is palpable, indeed virtually irresistible. The collective motivational well seems bottomless. The speed of effective change increases exponentially. Collective capacity, quite simply, gets more and deeper things done in shorter periods. (p. 72)

Building collective capacity implies that people take the opportunity to do things differently. They opt to learn new skills and to generate more effective practice *together* through mutual support, mutual accountability, and mutual challenge.

Purposeful collaboration is one way of ensuring that there is coherence and centrality of purpose within any change process.

> How would you rate your organization's current and potential capacity for growth and improvement?
>
> How far is your organization actively building the collective capacity for sustainable change and improvement?

The evidence from the top performing education systems around the world shows that for an improvement journey to be sustained over the long term, "improvements have to be integrated into the very fabric of the system pedagogy and that establishing collaborative practices is a central component of improvement in the long term" (Mourshed, Chijioke, & Barber, 2010, p. 11).

In their work, Sharratt and Fullan (2009, p. 9) suggest that the foundations of capacity building are as follows:

- Commitment to a shared vision and staying the course with a single priority
- Knowledge of and resources for focused assessment linked to instruction at all levels
- Strategic leadership emanating simultaneously and consistently from the center and the locality
- Engagement of parents and community involvement

Another perspective on capacity building is provided by Corcoran and Goertz (1995, p. 27). They point out that the term also relates to "the maximum or optimum amount of production and in so doing relates to issues of efficiency—the 'optimal amount of production that can be obtained from a given set of resources and organisational arrangements.'" This view sees capacity in terms of a better process (efficiency) and better outcomes (effectiveness). This must prompt any school or district leader to think about how capacities can be built so that teaching and learning processes are more efficient and the outcomes from schooling are improved. It must also necessitate some careful thought about the nature and effectiveness of professional learning.

In his work, Elmore (2002) argues that professional learning should be construed as a "collective good rather than a private or individual good, and its value should be judged by what it contributes to the individual's capacity to improve and the quality of instruction in the school and school system" (p. 14). The implication here is that professional development should *directly* contribute to not only individual improvement but also organizational improvement.

But effective professional learning cannot simply be a matter of routinely updating or up-skilling teachers. For professional learning to have an impact, then systematic and sustained professional collaboration is needed (Lieberman, 2009). When collaboration happens systematically, the group can "produce powerful results on an on-going basis" (Fullan, 2010b, p. 36). But exactly what form does this systematic professional collaboration take?

Many researchers and writers have outlined the potential of professional learning communities (PLCs) as a powerful means of systematic collaborative learning. Looking at the literature makes it clear that under the right conditions, effective professional communities can positively impact learner outcomes.

> *A number of large-scale studies have identified specific ways in which professional community-building can deepen teachers' knowledge, build their skills and improve instruction* (Darling-Hammond et al., 2009, p. 11).

The next chapter focuses on professional learning communities as one form of effective professional learning. It explores the different interpretations of PLCs and focuses on how PLC embody and exemplify distributed leadership in practice.

7

Distributed Leadership: Professional Learning Communities

The new paradigm for professional development for teachers lies in collaborative, participatory communities that enable teachers to learn and grow professionally, together

(Lemke, 2009, p. 13)

More than two decades ago, the organizational theorist, Peter Drucker (1988), identified what he called the *new organization*. This new organization consisted of a flat hierarchical structure. It was filled with skilled and motivated professionals who were part of innovative and flexible teams. Although the idea of distributed leadership was not in vogue then, the conception of the flatter more flexible structure fits exactly with contemporary thinking about leadership as extended influence. Since the introduction of the "new organisation" many other influential writers have elaborated upon Drucker's original idea, emphasizing that fluid and flexible teams are more creative and produce leadership that is more effective than that represented by more traditional hierarchical leadership structures (Weick, 2001).

Flatter structures and flexible teams have also been advocated by scholars writing about effective professional learning (DuFour & Eaker, 1998). These authors advocate that where teachers work in self-managing teams to develop goals, curricula, instructional strategies, and staff development programs, students can achieve at higher levels. The idea of team learning is a critically important feature of distributed leadership as its central premise is one of leading collaboratively in order to learn collectively.

In 2009, Linda Darling-Hammond and her colleagues undertook a major study for the National Staff Development Council that looked at the quality and nature of professional development in a range of countries including the United States. The report noted:

The United States is squandering a significant opportunity to leverage improvements in teacher knowledge to improve school and student performance. Other nations, our competitors, have made support for teachers and teachers' learning a top priority with significant results. In these countries, students learn and achieve more. Teachers stay in the field longer and are more satisfied with their work. Educators take on even more responsibility. (Darling-Hammond et al., 2009, p. 3)

*Effective professional development is intensive, ongoing, and con-
nected to practice; focuses on the teaching and learning of specific
academic content; is connected to other school initiatives and builds
strong working relationships among teachers.*

*Most teachers in the United States do not have access to professional
development that uniformly meets all these criteria.*

Source: Darling-Hammond et al., (2009, p. 5).

Around the globe, every year, teachers routinely participate in hundreds of hours of professional development and
training. The implicit assumption is that attending courses
equates with professional learning and that by participating
in these events somehow professional practice will change.
Now, without question, there are some good courses, powerful programs, and effective professional learning sessions.
But the return on this large-scale investment, in the form of
improved professional practice that leads to better learning
outcomes, is still highly questionable. There are a number of
key reasons.

First, many professional learning programs or courses operate on the assumption that knowledge gained from a "workshop" can be readily transferred into the "workplace." In other
words, it's assumed that ideas, knowledge, and skills gained in
one situation can be readily applied to another. Conversely, evidence would suggest that changes in professional behavior or
classroom practice are more likely to result from job-embedded
learning or learning in context. Second, teachers still tend to go
to external training or professional development events alone.
They experience the training independently, and however good
that training might be, the chances of convincing colleagues
back at schools of its merits will be low. It is like telling someone about a really good film that you watched. Secondhand, it
simply doesn't have the same impact.

Third, much depends on the quality of the training and its relevance to the participating teacher or teachers. Much of the professional learning field is still driven by commercial interest where profitability rather than applicability is the main goal. Consequently, the latest fads or fashions are quickly repackaged, marketed, and made available to teachers, not because they are the best thing but simply because they are the latest thing. Finally, and probably most importantly, there is still a predominant view that professional learning is primarily about the teacher and not the learner. Now, clearly, the teacher is important, as this is where professional expertise resides, but the focus or endpoint of professional learning should be the learner.

Can you imagine a doctor or dentist attending a training session on the use of a new drug or technique and then choosing not to apply that learning for the direct benefits of his or her patients? That would seem ludicrous. But so often, that is exactly what happens with so much professional learning and development. Teachers engage with the training, possibly enjoy it and even learn from it, fill in the happy sheet, and leave. It is as if the training is the end in itself rather than a means to an end. Now, I can hear you say, "But there are many programs, courses, and training sessions that are not like this. They *are* focused on the learner and not just the teacher." Yes, but They are still in relatively short supply. There is still far too much professional learning *without* impact. There is still too much professional development that makes little, if any, difference to the classroom.

PROFESSIONAL LEARNING WITH IMPACT

So what does professional learning with impact look like, necessitate, and require? If you were to ask this question, as I have, of many teachers in many schools in many countries, the short answer is not a professional course, not an external program, not even a master's degree. There is still little independent evidence to corroborate that these forms of professional development or training result in sustained improvement in professional practice. They can develop knowledge and understanding for sure but rarely change practice. Conversely, timely and appropriate guidance from another colleague or colleagues can be a powerful force for change. Time and time again, this is the response that school and district leaders give when asked the question, "What has influenced your professional practice most?" It comes down to the advice from trusted peers, colleagues, and in some cases those outside their school or district.

While this would naturally lead you to think that "coaching or mentoring" is the answer to professional learning with impact, think again. In the United States and other countries, a great deal of emphasis is placed upon mentoring and coaching as a productive use of valuable professional learning time. However, many claims that mentoring or coaching can result in improved professional practice simply remain unsubstantiated (Darling-Hammond et al., 2009).

There are studies which show that when the mentoring or coaching activities have a clear instructional focus, this interaction can enhance teacher performance, for example, where literacy coaches are used specifically to improve the teaching of literacy in schools in a "hands-on" way. The important point here is that the coaches have a clear instructional focus and an expertise that can be shared with others. Where this is not the case, then coaching or mentoring can free-fall into low-level guidance and support.

Where coaching or mentoring is "content-free" and represents a form of quasi counseling, the net effect will be zero, in terms of positive changes in instructional practice or student achievement. Teachers may feel better, but this may be the only outcome.

A major literature review, conducted as part of an Institute for Education Sciences evaluation of the Reading First program, reported mixed findings on the impact of coaching on improving instructional practice. It was noted that unless the instructional practices promoted through the processes of mentoring or coaching are *in and of themselves effective*, then a positive impact on teaching and learning is unlikely.

The substantive issue here is that if coaching or mentoring amounts to little more than a two-way "conversation," even if it is about learning, then once again, the benefits claimed for this form of professional learning will not be fully realized. If coaching and mentoring is unfocused and unstructured, it is unlikely to change professional practice for the better. To be most effective, coaching and mentoring has to have instructional knowledge at its core and have improving learner outcomes as the prime purpose and outcome of such professional collaboration.

If a "learning conversation," whether in the guise of mentoring or coaching, is to really change practice, it will require much more than simply sharing or processing ideas or questions through mutual reflection or discussion. Even with clear guidelines or rubrics, much will depend upon the level of expertise of those participating in the conversation and their skill at being able to analyze, reflect, and co-construct through mutual dialogue. If unfocused and unstructured, a learning conversation could prove to be little more than enthusiastic sharing of information and ideas among colleagues with zero learning and zero results.

In contrast, compared to other forms of professional learning, professional learning communities (PLCs) have significantly more empirical support. But before we take a look at the evidence base, it is important to be clear about terminology. What is a professional learning community?

WHAT'S IN A NAME?

The term *professional learning community* appears like confetti throughout the professional learning literature and like confetti, while attractive, can be devoid of substance. As Fullan (2010a) points out, "There has been a great deal written about professional learning communities . . . the term travels a lot better than the concept" (p. 36). Part of the reason for the different views of professional learning communities resides in the fact that there are shifts between different interpretations. There is a real conceptual muddle around PLCs.

> The term is used to describe two distinctively different things. A PLC can mean the entire organisation or a subgroup or team within the organisation. Used interchangeably, confusion naturally arises.

For example, in her work, Morrissey (2000, pp. 3–4) defines a professional learning community:

A school that operates as such engages the entire group of *professionals* in coming together for *learning* within a supportive, self-created *community*. Teacher and administrator learning is more complex, deeper, and more fruitful in a social setting, where the participants can interact, test their ideas, challenge their inferences and interpretations, and process new information with each other. The professional learning community provides a setting that is richer and more stimulating.

There are few that would argue with this definition of a *whole-school* PLC or the intentions behind it. As Stoll (2012, p. 6) proposes, "Professional learning communities are groups of teachers or school leaders, or even whole schools or groups of schools—also known as learning networks or networked learning communities." This definition is inclusive and expansive. It allows for wide participation and varied involvement. This interpretation is essentially derived from the concept of the "learning organization" where active participation of all stakeholders is an essential feature (Senge, 1990). For some writers, therefore, a PLC is simply a shorthand way of describing the cultural norms, values, and attributes of a learning organization. This interpretation of a PLC, as a whole organization, often describes what should be *aspired to* rather than what is *in place.*

For other writers, a PLC is a dynamic group or team that operates *within* a school or district, initially (Harris & Jones, 2012). Here the PLC is a collaborative group or team charged with the responsibility of improving the outcomes of a specific group of learners. The PLC is essentially a means of changing professional practice in order to improve learner outcomes. It is expected to take inquiry, innovate, and disseminate. Here, the professional learning community is a group of connected and engaged professionals who are responsible for driving instructional change and improvement within their organization first and foremost.

At the organizational level, the PLC is used to define *a schoolwide culture* that is focused upon building and sustaining school improvement. As such, PLCs can be composed of teachers, administrators, and support staff, and in some schools, PLCs are extended to community members and students (Stoll, Bolam, McMahon, Wallace, & Thomas, 2006; Stoll & Seashore Louis, 2007). In summary, the literature that focuses on the whole school or district as a professional learning community reinforces that it is characterized by teachers and administrators working collectively (Hord, 1997). It is a strategy to increase student achievement through creating a collaborative school culture focused on learning.

Conversely, the "within-school or-district" PLC, involves a collaborative team or teams focused on removing the barriers to learning. It has been defined as a "group of people sharing and critically interrogating their practice in an ongoing, reflective, collaborative, inclusive learning-oriented and growth-promoting way" (Waters & Cameron, 2003, p. 15).

> The job of a PLC can be summed up in three words: "improving learner outcomes" (Harris & Jones, 2010, p. 2).

The greatest advocates of PLCs in the United States interpret PLCs as a way of improving specific learner achievement and outcomes. In their view, a PLC is a group of "educators committed to working collaboratively in an on-going processes [*sic*] of collective inquiry and action research to achieve better results for the students . . . they serve" (DuFour, DuFour & Eaker, 2009).

"Within school or intra-school collaboration, in the form of professional learning teams or communities, when it is focused, produces results on an ongoing basis" (Fullan, 2010a, p. 36)

Professional learning communities, in the form of groups or teams within the organization, emanates directly from the idea of communities of practice (Wenger, 2000). Communities of practice are groups of people who share a passion for something they do and learn how to do it more effectively as they interact regularly and learn together. Over time, the members of the community develop a strong team identity; they develop personal relationships and establish ways of interacting, inquiring, and learning collectively. A community of practice defines itself along three dimensions—mutual engagement, shared repertoire, and joint enterprise (Wenger, 1998). These three dimensions also underpin effective PLCs and guide their collective action.

By definition, communities of practice comprise those who *share* professional expertise. The strength of a professional learning community is its combined professional practice and its common expertise. A professional learning team is a group with the norms of shared purpose, collective expertise, and an absolute focus on improving learner outcomes. While the views of different stakeholders are undoubtedly important, and might be sought to inform the work of the PLC, there is no requirement for their involvement within a PLC. Some would argue that involving outside agencies and stakeholders, as part of a whole-school

PLC, serves only to dilute the potential for meaningful change, as there are multiple agendas and perspectives to accommodate and address.

The many articles, books, and websites[1] devoted to PLCs largely and predictably promote their positive aspects. But there are some questions, particularly about the whole-school or district PLC that are rarely discussed or acknowledged. By definition, the features or characteristics of a PLC have been derived from organizations that are already high performing and effective. Researchers have distilled the essential features of high performing organizations and collectively described them as a PLC.

But it is not clear exactly how diagnosis converted into prescription. Rather like the school effectiveness research base (Chapman et al, 2012) which produced its ten or eleven characteristics of effective schools, somewhere this retrospective analysis of effectiveness was repackaged into prospective guidance. Put simply, the outputs of effective organizational performance (i.e., those that characterize a PLC[2]) have been repositioned as inputs and are held up to be the necessary prerequisites and requirements of improved organizational performance. While this indeed may be the case, the literature is less clear on exactly how to operationalize these inputs to create a PLC.

Without question, every school or district wants to be a rich, stimulating learning environment. But moving a school or district to function as a professional learning community is easier said than done. Transforming a school or a district into a PLC can be a huge and, potentially, impossible challenge. These are large units of change and realistically are too

---

[1] http://www.centerforcsri.org/plc.

[2] Traits of an effective PLC are shared values and vision, collaborative culture, focus on examining outcomes to improve student learning, supportive and shared leadership, and shared personal practice.

complex and too unwieldy to move in unison toward the goals of a PLC. Highly successful organizations invest in team building and create strategic opportunities for collective creativity (Collins & Hansen, 2011). The main point here is that while an entire organization can certainly aspire to be a learning community, this can only be achieved in reality through building an infrastructure of focused, sustained, and collaborative teamwork.

Organizations cannot automatically self-combust into a professional learning community however hard they try or strongly believe in the features of a PLC. The many sources of guidance including PLC simulations, checklists, and case studies serve only to underline that converting PLC outputs into PLC inputs is a zero-sum game. As the remainder of this book will argue, organizational improvement and high performance depends on a coordinated and disciplined approach to professional learning where leadership is distributed widely and wisely (see Chapter 8).

> The superintendent should focus district efforts on team based instructional improvement. The focus of team meetings should be the improvement of instruction, with the sharing of student achievement data. District leaders should provide time for teams to meet and review performance on a consistent basis. (Horton & Martin, 2013, p. 58)

Within the literature, not only do definitions and explanations of PLCs vary in interpretation, but they can also wander, even between the pages of the same book or article. So returning to the PLC as a team, it is important to be clear about what this actually looks like within a school or district. It is also important that the PLC is not confused with a working party, subgroup, or committee. If this occurs, there will be a new label for existing practice, but the status quo will remain.

So when is a PLC not a PLC?

A PLC	Not a PLC
Group of professionals working as a cohesive team to address specific learner needs arising from an analysis of data and evidence.	Formally established or existing sub or working group with a remit for an existing theme, subject, or topic.
Chooses the focus of inquiry and the membership of the group.	Prescribed focus and membership (e.g., a working party is given its task or brief).
Imperative to generate new ideas and new practice.	Expectation of sharing existing knowledge, information, or practice.
Operates within a clear cycle of action inquiry.	Inquiry is not an expectation.
Leadership is widely distributed, and the group chooses its own facilitator.	There is a designated or preexisting leader of the group.
Each member is accountable for the outcomes of the PLC—there is reciprocal accountability.	One person is responsible for producing minutes, sharing the outcomes, reporting, and so on.
Disbands and reforms with a new focus on inquiry and changed membership.	Continued membership and work of established group is ongoing.
Assesses its impact directly on learner outcomes and has a responsibility to share these outcomes with others.	Engages in reporting and written dissemination.
Independent and interdependent learning.	Dependent learning.
Reflection upon individual and collective learning based on evidence.	Reports on group progress.
Community of learners.	Cooperative participants.
Collective capacity building.	Consensual group working.

Now that some definitional issues are resolved, let's return to the actual evidence. The evidence about the impact on organizational change and improvement of intraorganizational professional learning communities[3] as highlighted above is fairly consistent. A summary of the main findings is as follows:

- Professional learning communities (PLCs) have a positive impact on *student achievement* (Dufour, Dufour, Eaker, & Karhanek, 2010; Goldenberg, 2004; Saunders, Goldenberg, & Gallimore, 2009; Stoll et al., 2006; Verscio, Ross, & Adams, 2008; Whitehurst, 2002).
- A PLC enables teachers to engage in collaborative inquiry and change within their own schools *initially* and across schools subsequently (Dufour et al., 2009).
- A PLC is a powerful vehicle for changing teachers' behavior and improving student learning outcomes but only when it is focused on the *improvement of learning* rather than the improvement of teaching (DuFour & Eaker, 1998; Little, 1990).
- Teachers who are part of a professional learning community within their school tend to be more effective in the classroom and *achieve better student outcomes* (Huffman & Jacobson, 2003; Lewis & Andrews, 2004).
- Teacher inquiry is at the heart of effective professional learning communities; it is a key driver in improving *classroom practice* (Bielaczyc & Collins, 1999; Harris & Jones, 2010, 2012; Hopkins, 2002)
- Professional learning communities improve teachers' professional learning and secure improved *school performance,* irrespective of the school context and its socioeconomic profile (Elmore, 2002; Stoll et al., 2006)
- Professional learning communities can enhance professionalism and prevent stress and burnout. They provide a forum to translate research into practice in the classroom (Rosenholz, 1989).

---

[3]This is the result when it is properly established, focused, and organized, that is, when disciplined and systematic.

Professional learning communities have been shown to lead to increased involvement, ownership, innovation, and leadership among teachers (Lewis & Andrews, 2004; Berry, Johnson, & Montgomery, 2005; Sargent & Hannum, 2009). In addition, they offer a means or a mechanism for developing, supporting, and enhancing distributed leadership practice. With such compelling evidence about the impact of PLCs, it would be hard to think of a reason why those working in schools and districts would not want to develop them. But can PLCs work at scale? And to what degree are they a feature of high performance in sectors other than education?

PLCs and High Performance

In downtown Boston, a dot–com business specializes in selling shoes on line. It is called ShoeBuy.com, and it is featured in a contemporary study of organizations that *perform beyond expectations* (Hargreaves et al., 2010). It is fascinating in many respects notwithstanding the idea that people would actually buy their shoes online! When it was established, other dot–com companies were riding the dot–com boom, and ShoeBuy. com was growing at a steady rate. After the meltdown in Silicon Valley, ShoeBuy.Com was one of a small number of dot–com companies that weathered the storm. Its survival was explained by its CEO in two ways. First, the company had resisted expanding too quickly; they waited when others rushed greedily ahead. Second, they worked as a strong, virtual professional community.

Inevitably, those working for a dot–com company are unlikely to be housed together in the same building, the same town, or even the same country. They are unlikely to be with other colleagues at the same time or indeed any time! The virtual world affords twenty-four-hour working possibilities, and face-to-face collaboration is therefore not a strong option in high tech environments. What characterises ShoeBuy.Com and many of the other businesses in the Performance Beyond

Expectations (PBE) study was the fact that they operate as a strong community of professionals who work and learn together. The leaders of PBE organizations cultivated a strong sense of belonging, a fraternity among members that reinforced a very potent sense of collective identity (Hargreaves et al., 2010).

Scott Bader, another of the business sites in the study, was a "not-for-profit" organization established on clear cooperative values. It reinforced the importance of community within the organization but also prioritized the wider community by its charitable and altruistic contributions. The CEO talked about the company as a "family" that worked together, that shared the same values and principles. The culture of the organization was cohesive, and it was this factor alone which allowed them to face difficult decisions together. While the external economic environment placed the company under extreme pressure, they were able to survive and subsequently perform at an exceptional level because of one important factor: community.

While the companies in the PBE study did not know the term, they were encouraging and supporting professional learning communities or teams that drove innovation and change within the organization. All the high performing businesses espoused a strong team spirit and established teams within their organization to collaborate as well as compete. In essence, their teams exhibited all the characteristics and dimensions of a PLC. For example, they worked together to solve problems, enjoyed mutual trust and respect, and practiced reciprocal accountability and pressure to innovate so that the whole organization would benefit. The core idea behind professional learning communities or teams is that they operate as a catalyst *within* an organization to secure change and improvement. They have a central responsibility for generating new ideas and practices so that organizational outcomes improve. They can also drive change at scale.

An increasing number of examples exist of large-scale system improvement involving professional learning communities. In Canada, there are two such examples that highlight the way in which PLCs can mobilize change and improvement. The first example is in Ontario and the second example is the York Region District School Board in Toronto (Fullan, 2011a; Sharrat & Fullan, 2009). In both cases, the process of large-scale improvement paid attention to building a powerful infrastructure for professional learning and change. In Ontario, the four key organization supports for change were the following:

- Engagement and commitment by the adults in the system
- Effective collective processes for educators to continue to improve their practices (often referred to as professional learning communities)
- Aligned, coherent, and supportive system policies and practices
- Appropriate allocation of resources (Sharrat & Fullan, 2009, p. 13)

In Toronto, the main levers of change were the following:

- Using data to drive instruction and the selection of resources
- Building administrators' and teachers' capacity for focused literacy assessment and literacy instruction
- Establishing professional learning communities across all schools to share successful practice (Sharrat & Fullan, 2009, p. 14)

Across the Atlantic in a much smaller country, a major reform effort is underway to improve the entire education system. Change is taking place at school, district, and government levels in order to secure higher performance and improved learner outcomes. Substantial effort is being put into building the capacity for large-scale reform in a deliberate and purposeful way. A concerted effort is being made in Wales to improve professional practice through the large-scale adoption of professional learning communities within, between, and across schools. Although still in the early stages of implementation, evidence would suggest that professional learning communities in Wales are creating the collective leadership capacity for change and improvement that ultimately will make a difference to learner outcomes (Harris & Jones, 2012).

> The development of leadership capacity is essential to the transformation of our educational systems. (Horton & Martin, 2013, p. 56)

The main message here is that developing leadership capacity, particularly at scale, does not happen by default but has to be purposefully crafted, designed, and carefully implemented. In the case of Canada, Wales, and many of the high performing Southeast Asian counties, PLCs are being actively used as the architecture for generating collective capacity building and improvement (Harris et al., 2013). PLCs have been selected primarily because the evidence shows that as a way of improving outcomes, they actually work. In other words, where there is a clear model or a methodology that consistently supports professional collaboration, there is much greater chance of success.

DISCIPLINED COLLABORATION

In the remaining part of this book, it will be argued that distributed leadership in the form of professional collaboration has to be *disciplined* to be effective. Without a clear model and a modus operandi, there is a real danger that professional collaboration will lapse into low-level "groupthink" or weak consensus with glowing but unsubstantiated accounts of impact. So often, I hear comments such as "The collaborative work had impact because teachers reported positive changes in the classroom" or "The collaborative work has made a difference in the district as teachers say that they now communicate more and share materials between schools." On the report card of change and innovation, these statements may score 10 for enthusiasm, but there is relatively little evidence of the impact upon student learning.

The absence of any substantive discussion about professional collaboration and impact can be explained in two ways. First, thoughts about the impact of professional learning are usually post hoc, retrospectively conjured up by asking teachers what they thought or felt the impact might be. Second, models of professional collaboration or professional learning rarely include impact assessment in their design or delivery. Possibly, this explains why "the profession, its knowledge base lag woefully behind the demands placed on schools, teachers students and society" (Cordingley, 2013, p. 3).

Many would argue that not every professional learning experience or professional development program can or, indeed, should demonstrate an impact on student learning. True. But then why on earth invest in it in the first place? Surely, the whole point of professional learning is to bring about positive change in the classroom, to improve learning, to have an impact on learners? Otherwise what are we actually doing? If we are serious about changing things in schools and districts rather than simply rearranging them, then it is imperative to invest in the most powerful forms of professional learning (PL), i.e. those that make a difference to student learning. This takes us right back to professional learning communities.

> Effective work based PL involves teachers openly making their continuing learning evident to their students on a sustained basis through active, and increasingly self directed learning activities that are structured and scaffolded by evidence. (Cordingley, 2013, p. 5)

One example of effective work-based PL is within-school professional learning communities where there is a commitment to continue developing practice and to experiment with new pedagogical processes. PLC work that is properly focused means that students have the chance to observe professional collaboration and to experience changes in pedagogy and practice firsthand. While there are many versions of a research-based approach to professional collaboration, the following seven-stage model, is currently being used within, between, and across schools to secure a positive change in learner outcomes (Harris & Jones, 2010). It is outlined here simply to show one potential model that schools or districts can use to inform and support their PLC work.

PROFESSIONAL LEARNING COMMUNITIES IN ACTION

This model suggests that a within-school or district PLC has seven interrelated stages that combine to provide the basis for effective professional collaborative working. The first stage and second stage are interchangeable as it could be the case that the issue or problem is so clear that a group is easily identified and quickly established to deal with it. Conversely, a focus of inquiry may be identified from an analysis of data at the school or district level; then, the group is established.

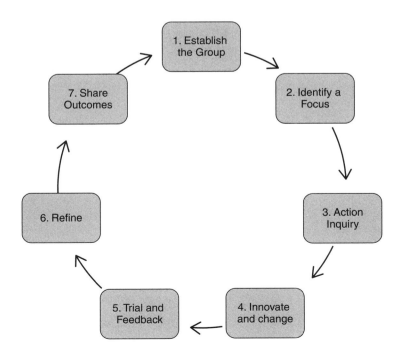

Having established its particular *focus of inquiry*, the PLC group then engages in a research or inquiry process to obtain further information and to locate potential solutions or alternative practices. On the basis of the analysis of the findings from the inquiry stage, an innovation or intervention is selected or designed by the group and subsequently used in a classroom trial. Data are collected about the implementation and impact of the innovation or intervention. On the basis of the data or feedback, modifications or refinements are made. The innovation or intervention is then put to the test of practice once again. The outcomes and recommendations from the group are then shared more widely with others within the school in order to inform their professional knowledge and practice.

There are two key activities that drive this seven-stage PLC model. These are meaningful **collaboration and active inquiry**. Within effective PLCs, professionals work together in a collaborative way, with an emphasis on mutual inquiry, interrogation of data, and scrutiny of evidence in order to establish a specific focus for the PLC to address.

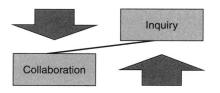

Effective PLC groups or teams engage in systematic processes of inquiry in order to secure improvement. Through robust self-evaluation, analysis of data, and analysis of evidence, members of the PLC can determine the pedagogical–instructional knowledge and skills required to improve outcomes.

Improvement, growth, and renewal are the main hallmarks of an effective professional learning community. Professional learning communities provide opportunities for staff to look deeply into the process of instruction and to learn how to become more effective in their work with students. But as Carmichael (1982, p. 12) maintains, "Students cannot raise their level of achievement until teachers become more effective in their own practice." Teachers can only become more effective in their own practice through disciplined collaboration and inquiry.

> In a school or district, an effective professional learning community is characterized by disciplined inquiry focused upon improving learner outcomes. It is not about teacher improvement; first and foremost, it is essentially about putting the learner first.
>
> Participants in a professional learning community are primarily there to seek new methods of supporting student learning, to put those methods to the test of practice, and then to refine and share based on their results.

DISCIPLINED COLLABORATION AND INQUIRY

Through focused and disciplined collaborative inquiry, professionals can identify an issue or problem that they want to work upon, gather evidence about it, and put together an intervention that they apply, test, and refine. Inquiry can take a variety of forms, for example, teachers could undertake a learning walk around the school to collect data on particular issues or topics; they could embark upon appreciative inquiry where the main purpose is to look for good practice; or they could participate in a guided inquiry which is a more structured and focused approach to action inquiry. Whatever *collaborative method* they choose, essentially it is a way of collecting evidence about an area for improvement or change or an approach to improvement and change.

Sharing professional knowledge, including the outcomes of collaborative inquiry and other research, can be challenging. What makes sense and works well for one group may not easily translate to others. Yet a critical part of the work of professional learning communities is sharing knowledge that might help enhance the practice of others. Consequently, systematic approaches to sharing and dissemination are needed so that they can illuminate new knowledge and allow those who have not been part of the professional learning community to engage with the ideas. In this respect, disciplined collaborative inquiry is not an end in itself but a means to an end.

> If professional learning communities are to be more than just a cooperative activity where participants feel good about themselves, then there has to be *reciprocal accountability*.
>
> Professional collaborative inquiry has to have a hard edge with tangible outcomes.
>
> It has to have an *impact*.

At best, professional learning communities offer a platform for mutual inquiry and learning. They offer teachers and district staff the ability to ask questions about their practice and the practice of others in a safe and trusting environment. They provide a basis for better and deeper communication between professionals as they undertake their inquiry. It is this deeper, collective reflection that will ultimately make a difference to learning and learner outcomes.

Professional learning communities are primarily concerned with generating new knowledge and new practice through sharing, collaboration, and joint inquiry. Whereas networks can offer support and circulate existing knowledge, conversely, a strong professional learning community can generate new knowledge and new learning (Harris & Jones, 2010). However, much depends on the way the PLC is led and supported. As noted earlier, formal leaders play an important role in making distributed leadership happen.

ROLE OF THE LEADER IN PLCS

The main role of the formal leader in supporting professional learning communities, as with any form of collaboration (see Chapter 8), is to create the time, the opportunity, and the resources for the group to function effectively. The leader creates the organizational conditions where the group can work together in an optimum way (see Chapter 8). In some cases, the leader might be part of the professional learning community to guide and support it but not to drive or lead it. As the professional learning community becomes more effective and sophisticated, the leader will probably no longer participate but will maintain oversight from afar.

The central role of the leader in a professional learning community therefore is to provide pressure and support, to ensure that the group works effectively, and to ensure that there are outcomes to show as a result of their collaboration (see Chapter 8). Lave and Wenger (1991, p. 25) propose that when learning in communities of practice, participants gradually absorb and are absorbed in a *culture of practice* giving them exemplars and leading to shared meanings, a sense of belonging, and increased understanding.

The collective responsibility that is at the heart of professional learning communities can be secured only if there is a culture of professional respect and trust. This directly relates to the earlier discussion about social capital and capacity building. The formal leader inevitably plays a pivotal role in setting the culture or climate of the organization and supporting collective inquiry and collaborative innovation. They are chiefly responsible for creating the internal conditions where professional learning communities can make a real difference or be little more than a low-level working group.

This is not to discount or dismiss issues of power or authority or to ignore the potential for the misuse of shared leadership in practice (Lumby, 2013). Those writing about distributed leadership have been fairly careful not to airbrush out the challenges of distributed leadership practice (Harris, 2009). Looking at the literature on distributed leadership makes clear that this is a highly contested idea and anyone familiar with the debates surrounding distributed leadership would find it impossible to conclude that it does little more than reinforce the "status quo" (Lumby, 2013). In addition, those writing about distributed leadership fully acknowledge that it is not immune from those more negative or destructive forces that any form of leadership encounters. As Chapter 5 showed, there is a dark side to any leadership practice, and distributed leadership certainly has its dark side.

Anyone working in a school or a district knows only too well the impact of gender and race on all educational processes, including leadership; they do not need to be told. Distributed leadership is not a free-for-all form of leadership or a subtle Machiavellian plot, as some would have us believe. It is a form of leadership that comprises not only shared responsibility but also shared accountability.

> Who gets to make decisions in your organization is the center of gravity for accountability (Ricci & Wiese, 2011).

But just creating communities of professionals does not guarantee meaningful change or improvement. Real improvement through professional learning communities means focusing on the needs of the learner first and working relentlessly to improve pedagogy so those needs are effectively met (Harris & Jones, 2010, 2011).

The most effective PLCs display or reflect certain characteristics.

- Clarity of focus—directly related to improving learner outcomes
- Consistent use of data to identify the focus and to monitor progress
- Collaboration of professionals with purpose
- Capacity building through the engagement and involvement of others
- Coherent action and change in pedagogical practice
- Communication of outcomes to other professionals
- Change in learner outcomes

How far do the PLCs in your school reflect these characteristics? Are there some characteristics that you would add to this list?

In summary, there are a number of important points of connection between distributed leadership and professional learning communities. First, distributed leadership is associated with the creation of *collegial norms* among professionals that can contribute directly to enhanced outcomes. Second, distributed leadership equates with giving professionals *opportunities to lead* so they can have a positive influence. Third, at its most practical level, distributed leadership means that professionals are *working as instructional leaders* influencing curriculum, teaching, and the professional practice of others.

It remains the case that the most effective professional learning communities or teams function well primarily because of the quality of support and challenge that they receive. There are very few examples of effective collaboration without focused leadership or facilitation. The next chapter introduces a model of disciplined collaboration and considers the challenges of leading effective professional collaboration.

Distributed Leadership: Professional Collaboration With Impact

The main point of collaboration is "to connect to learn" but often little thought is given to the establishment of those connections and scant attention is paid to the fact that to be most productive and effective, some professionals need to "learn to connect"

(Harris & Jones, 2012).

All too often, books about leadership tend toward theory or research or practice, rarely combining all these elements effectively or well. For some ideas, the theory–practice divide is there for very good reason. Some years ago, Howard Gardner reinforced that some theories cannot be and indeed should not be translated into practice. He was absolutely right. Multiple intelligence theory, in its lowest level of practical application, is little more than blatant commercialism and a misrepresentation of the original theoretical position.

In the field of educational leadership and administration, many have long lamented the research–practice divide. As Spillane and Coldren (2011, p. 108) note: "We contend that this divide is in part a reflection of the field's preoccupation with schools writ large rather than thinking systematically about leading and managing the core work of schools—teaching and learning." A central argument throughout this book has been that distributed leadership practice is connected to changing the "technical core" of teaching and learning and that this change is most likely to be effective from focused and disciplined professional collaboration.

Unlike multiple intelligence theory, there is a clear relationship between distributed leadership theory, research, and practice. It can be explained quite simply—distributed leadership theory talks about *multiple or collective influences.* The distributed leadership research shows that multiple or collective influences can, under the right conditions, *positively influence organizational outcomes.* Distributed leadership practice reinforces that *professional collaboration* can generate effective collective influence that results in change and innovation.

Many would argue that the prime aim of leadership in the 21st century is innovation. Using a distributed leadership frame, innovation is generated through sharing and collaboration. But if you were to ask a dozen management gurus to define innovation, you would probably get a dozen different answers. It is a slippery concept and one that lends itself to much misinterpretation. Peter Drucker defines innovation as "a change that creates a new dimension of performance." This definition comes closest to elucidating the core purpose of professional collaboration. It is centrally about creating change that will have an impact; it is about learning to do things differently in order to positively effect outcomes.

As Hargreaves (2003) points out,

> Innovation is a delicate plant, which thrives in a favourable climate. It grows in stages. It begins with the perception that something needs to change, stimulating bright ideas about what might be done. Each idea is elaborated and put to an early test, and then dropped because it proves to be deficient or further supported because it promises to work. Once proved, it is disseminated to those people or places where it can be used to advantage. (p. 33)

In essence, there are three dimensions to innovation:

- Problem finding
- Creating solutions
- Generating knowledge

These dimensions accord with the three stages of the approach to professional collaboration introduced in this chapter. The disciplined collaboration model (see Appendix) has three stages—implementation, innovation, and impact. The evidence shows that the most effective collaborative team or professional learning communities are not those that seek solutions to focus their efforts on self-evident problems. Instead, they collectively inquire and investigate in order to highlight a problem to address in imaginative and new ways. Effective collaborative teams or PLCs are problem seeking and not problem solving.

Highlighting a problem and subjecting it to the test of practice requires creativity and risk taking. But it also requires *discipline*. If collaborative working is to be truly innovative, it also has to be rigorous and adopt a consistent and systematic methodology (see Appendix). However, systematic does not mean systematized, with implications of control and routinized behavior. Rather, systematic means that the professional collaboration is focused, carefully planned, and ultimately focused on generating new ideas, understanding, and knowledge.

But new ways of learning don't just happen. New professional learning necessitates trying something out, working at it, feeling uncomfortable for a while, and adapting practice as a result. It means struggling with ambiguity and pressing forward even in the face of criticism or confusion because there are barriers to student learning that need to be addressed. In this respect, professional collaboration is far from a soft option or cozy consensus. It requires focus, patience, and ultimately "discipline" to make it happen most effectively. This final chapter draws upon advice and guidance to support disciplined collaborative learning (Harris and Jones, 2012 & Jones, 2013) (Jones, 2013). Some of the pages have been reproduced in the Appendix to support leaders in schools and districts, to support their collaborative work.

Often, I am asked "How do I make distributed leadership happen in practice? What are the key steps?" While there are no neat formulas or easy ring binder solutions that can help address these questions, although I am sure some have been proposed and written, there are certain things that can be practically done to make distributed leadership authentic. One practical way forward, as this book has argued and illustrated, is to create strong collaborative teams or professional learning communities where leadership is naturally and authentically distributed. The evidence about group learning is clear—purposeful and focused collaboration is a skill that has to be acquired, repeated, and practiced in context. In professional collaboration, the learning belongs to the group; it is a collective enterprise. However, for any social learning process to be effective, some scaffolding and structure is required.

To be most effective, teams have to learn the skills of collaboration. They have to practice collective ways of working together, and they have to establish clear norms and rules of engagement. They have to *learn to connect*. The evidence about group learning reinforces that purposeful and focused collaboration is a skill that has to be acquired, repeated, and practiced in context. It is skill that benefits from the guidance, pressure, and support of a facilitator.

Within collaborative learning, the facilitator role is one of support for *peer-to-peer collaboration and inquiry*. Not only will each PLC, or collaborative team, require its own internal facilitator, but it will also benefit from some external facilitation when additional expertise, support, or advice is needed. The facilitator is there to offer a careful balance of support and challenge. Facilitation is also important to ensure that leadership is genuinely distributed and that the work of the group does not degenerate into low-level consensus or ineffectual groupthink.

The research on effective collaborative learning shows

1. the skills of collaboration have to be modeled, practiced, and refined and
2. effective collaboration requires high-quality intervention and facilitation.

Facilitation is the process of taking a group through a process of learning or change in a way that encourages each member of the group to participate and to play an active part. Without focused coordination and support, group members can easily opt out or become "passengers" in the collaborative inquiry process. To avoid this possibility, any collaborative group or team will need purposeful and consistent facilitation to ensure a maximum return on their collective time and effort.

To be most effective, a facilitator will need to recognize that each person has something unique and valuable to share with the group. The facilitator's role is to elicit *existing* knowledge and ideas from different members of a group, to help encourage them to learn from each other, to think and act together, and to generate *new* knowledge and ideas that can be shared with others. This new knowledge does not have to be revolutionary or groundbreaking but can simply represent a departure from existing practice or a small but significant change.

FACILITATING COLLABORATIVE LEARNING

Effective facilitation is about empowering other professionals to learn both individually and collectively. It involves letting go of control over the outcome of a process and giving that responsibility to the group. It is not about leading or driving the group, but the role requires the ability to stand back and guide collective learning. This can prove to be a challenge, particularly if there is a wish to see immediate results. Effective collaborative inquiry takes time. Therefore, the real skill of facilitation is knowing how and when to intervene. If the collaborative inquiry process is to lead to meaningful change that is sustainable, this will be achieved only if strong, trusting relationships are forged within the group and the group owns its own learning process.

An effective facilitator will also have certain personal characteristics that encourage all group members to actively participate in the learning process. These characteristics include empathy, humility, generosity, and patience, combined with understanding, acceptance, and affirmation. An effective facilitator also needs certain skills and abilities. Facilitation skills are essential for anyone who is seeking to lead others in a participatory process of discussion, learning, and change. If the collaborative learning and inquiry process is to be owned by the team or alliance, it needs to be clear within the group and agreed on exactly what the role of the facilitator is and is not.

The skill of the facilitator will vary due to the varying degrees of maturity in professional learning exhibited by each group, different phases in building a collaborative team or group, the characteristics and culture of the collaborative group, the attitude or approach of the formal leadership to collaborative working, the focus or purpose of the collaborative team, and the internal–external facilitator relationship. Facilitation will also vary due to the differences between schools or districts in terms of their understanding of collaborative learning and inquiry. It will also vary depending upon which stage of the connect to learn (C2L) model is being supported (Jones, 2013; see Appendix).

- **Implementation**—the facilitator's role is to build trust, to establish norms or ways of working, and to secure a shared focus of inquiry and a methodology for exploring that focus.
- **Innovation**—the facilitator's role is to keep up momentum, to ensure that innovation is taking place and that this is subsequently trailed, refined, and shared with others.
- **Impact**—the facilitator's role is to ensure throughout the collaborative process that impact is captured at each stage and that there is evidence to share and disseminate with others outside the group.

So let's go to a real school and look at part of this process in action. The following excerpt is taken from the work of Spillane and Coborn (2011, pp. 10–11) as an illustration of the way in which *diagnosis and design* were part of the leadership practice at the school. It also exemplifies, really well, the start of a process of disciplined collaboration.

Baxter school, in Chicago, serves a culturally diverse student population that has been shifting in recent years, with 70% of Baxter's students qualifying for free or reduced lunch. Baxter's students performed well on the Iowa Test of Basic Skills with 60% scoring at or above national norms on the reading portion and 69% doing well on the mathematics portion. But when the principal took a closer look at the student achievement data and reanalysed it longitudinally to measure actual student growth over time, he identified some surprising grade and cohort level trends. Compared to the top 12 performing schools in the district, students at Baxter were at the bottom when it came to actual growth. The principal at Baxter marshalled these data

(Continued)

(Continued)

as evidence that all was not well at Baxter, defining the problem as one of stagnant growth in student achievement. He explained:

The **diagnosis** made clear that out of 12 schools Baxter was at the bottom or really close to the bottom in terms of the amount of actual growth. Forget about where the growth started, forget about the base, forget about the end. Just, you know how many months of progress, on average were 6th graders achieving at Baxter school? The principal did not simply tell teachers the cause of the stagnant student achievement. Rather he presented these **data** to the staff, grabbed their attention and challenged them to engage with him in diagnostic work to figure it out. Indeed student achievement data became a focal point of discussions in a variety of settings from grade level and faculty meetings to the school improvement process and guided conversations about curricular priorities and instructional improvement.

The more chances people have to talk, and not just in circles but talk about a common ground problems, the more comfortable they feel with change, and the better they get in their practice.

However, the school staff did not rely only on student data for their diagnostic work; they gathered additional data to identify as well. The school's literacy committee conducted classroom observations and teacher surveys and analysed *new* data to identify why student growth was flat. Nor did these data offer any clues as to what sort of redesign (**development**) efforts might be needed to reverse the trend. The surveys suggested a split between early and later primary teachers with respect to how they thought about reading instruction. A teacher member of the Literacy Committee noted:

We did a survey of the faculty . . . and what we discovered was that the teachers, after about 2nd or 3rd grade, didn't think of themselves as teache[r]s of reading at all. It was like they teach that in 1st or 2nd grade and now I am teaching my subject, my content area. She went on to say that—we saw the pattern emerging that people didn't consider themselves as teachers of reading and they didn't have a clue where to begin teaching reading . . . that was the beginning of our realisation that that was a problem area.

CODA

While Einstein might have discovered the theory of relativity by sitting alone in the lab, today's breakthroughs are much more likely to be the result of strongly connected, securely aligned, and sound collaborative practice. Companies have awakened to the power of collaboration and the "win-win" of collectively working together. Just as the initial emergence of the Internet disrupted everything, there is now another major shift taking place. In this ubiquitous networked world, collaboration technologies now connect distributed global teams. The technology that runs our lives is fast, open, decentralized, and highly adaptable.

Meeting the educational needs of the 21st century will require greater leadership capability and capacity than ever before within, between, and across schools. It will demand that formal leaders concentrate their efforts on developing the leadership capability and capacity of others, in both their school and other schools. But distributed leadership is not simply about creating more leaders. The steady accumulation of more and more leaders does not equate with distributed leadership. The issue is not one of increasing the numbers of leaders but rather one of increasing leadership quality and capability.

The "so what" of distributed leadership is the recognition that the core task of the formal leader is to support those with the expertise to lead, wherever they reside within the school or district. It is to judge when this expertise is needed for the development of the organization and to engage this expertise in an authentic and respectful way. The main challenge for formal leaders who want better performance and better outcomes is to actively build the leadership capacity within their organization, so that productive change and continuous improvement can become a real possibility. To build the leadership capacity within their school, formal leaders need to harness the collective will, skill, and leadership of all those in their organization in a carefully sequenced way so that the organization, as a whole, benefits (Harris, 2011b).

As the evidence shows, exceptional organizational performance is not a random event; instead, exceptional performance is achieved through careful planning, design, and "discipline" (Collins & Hansen, 2011). It requires organizational alignment, mutual understanding, and flexibility, rather than rigidity, prescription, or coercion. For formal leaders seeking improved organizational performance and better outcomes, the challenge is to create the conditions where professional knowledge and skills are enhanced, where effective leadership exists, at all levels, and where the entire organization is working interdependently in the collective pursuit of better outcomes.

But there are some challenges, as this book has highlighted. Distributed leadership implies shifts in power, authority, and control. Research by Arrowsmith (2012) provides some warning signals about distributed leadership from principals who felt an acute sense of personal accountability and responsibility for the school's performance. Ultimately, those at the apex of the organization will be judged based on the performance of their organization. This is a real tension and dilemma for those leaders who feel the weight of responsibility squarely on their shoulders, alone.

Another challenge concerns the issue of building relational trust so that distributed leadership is authentic and is not simply delegation by another name. Successful distribution of leadership depends upon the firm establishment of mutual trust—this is the glue that makes all highly effective organizations perform at the highest level. In their research findings, Day et al. (2011) reinforce that trust is essential for the progressive and effective distribution of leadership. They note that building and sustaining trust is a critical feature of highly effective school leaders and that without the ability to nurture trusting relationships, the potential to improve organizational performance will be dramatically reduced.

For school and district leaders who seek improved organizational performance and better outcomes, the challenge is to create the conditions where the entire organization is committed to working collectively and interdependently in order to achieve better outcomes. The evidence clearly points toward a collective solution where professionals work together to create new knowledge, to find new solutions, and to invent new pedagogy. Here, distributed leadership is an ecosystem that supports collective working and ensures the contribution of the many rather than the few. This is not to suggest that professional collaboration is the answer, alone. In the amalgam of school, district, and system reform, there are other important components. But without this collective capacity building, even the most well-thought-through reforms or interventions are unlikely to succeed (Fullan, 2010a).

In an era of greater accountability and ever more stringent measures of performance, those in formal leadership roles in schools and districts face a demanding and some would argue daunting task. In the pursuit of better outcomes for all young people, whatever their background, there are difficult decisions to make and many potential trades-offs to be considered. Distributed leadership does not guarantee better performance; it is not a panacea for success, it does not possess any innate good or bad qualities, it is not friend or foe. Much depends on the nature of distributed practice and the intentions behind it.

If distributed leadership is to make any real difference at all, one thing is certain: those in formal leadership positions in schools and districts have a substantial and integral role to play in making it happen.

> Our current leadership model is not sustainable. Transformed business models and faster information flows mean leadership styles need to change to become more collaborative. Now a leader is a person who sets the context, creates networks and can facilitate decision making at all levels within an organisation. If you are a leader today, be warned; what got you there may not necessarily keep you there. (Mitchell & Learmond, 2010, p. 4)

Appendix

CONNECT TO LEARN—C2L

The following pages are taken from *Connecting Professional Learning* (Harris and Jones, 2012) published by the National College for School Leadership in England. The intention of this resource was to support the collaborative work between schools. The C2L process is equally applicable to a "within-school" approach to professional collaboration as the stages are exactly the same, although the questions would need to reflect a group of individuals rather than a group of schools.

While it is not possible to reproduce the whole resource, the pages that follow are intended to support the work of those *leading or facilitating* the professional collaboration of others (see Chapter 8).

The basic components of the C2L model appear below, and while they are divided into the three phases of implementation, innovation, and impact, they are essentially interrelated, and collectively they reflect the elements of effective collaborative working.

Each phase has the same set of building blocks—outlined in the grids below. These are the following:

Diagnosis—Where are we? What are the main issues or problems we are facing?

✚ The Model

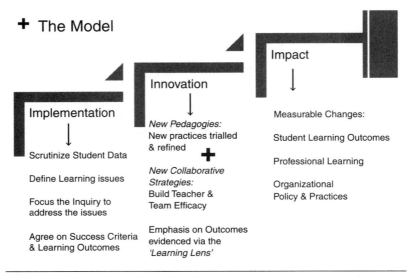

Impact

↓

Measurable Changes:

Student Learning Outcomes

Professional Learning

Organizational
Policy & Practices

Innovation

↓

New Pedagogies:
New practices trialled
& refined

✚

*New Collaborative
Strategies:*
Build Teacher &
Team Efficacy

Emphasis on Outcomes
evidenced via the
'Learning Lens'

Implementation

↓

Scrutinize Student Data

Define Learning issues

Focus the Inquiry to
address the issues

Agree on Success Criteria
& Learning Outcomes

Source: Copyright Harris and Jones (2012).

Data—How can we be sure that we are focusing on the real issue and how do we gauge our progress and impact?

Development—What strategy approaches are we trying? How well are they working?

Distributed Leadership—Are we working as a collaborative team? Are we truly sharing leadership?

Drive—Are we maintaining and sustaining our collaborative efforts? How do we keep things going? What needs to happen to ensure our work is embedded in the long term?

The diagnosis and development components are similar to Spillane and Coburn's (2011) *diagnosis and design* elements of distributed leadership. However, unlike their model, the C2L model focuses on outcomes as well as describing and capturing activity. It is deliberately constructed so that impact is thought about at the outset and not left to chance or retrofitted following the collaborative activity. The prime purpose of the C2L model is to ensure that professional collaboration has impact.

Phase One—IMPLEMENTATION—Facilitator's Overview		
Individual School		
	'Start Up Phase'	**Assessment**	**Facilitator Aide Memoire**
Diagnosis	When encountering a new school to be part of your collaborative group it will be important to diagnose the real, rather than perceived need. This diagnosis is important because it will allow you to gauge the needs of the individual schools versus the collective needs of the schools that intend to collaborate. Questions to ask: From your self-evaluation or other assessment(s), as a school what are the main priorities for school development? How do you intend to meet those priorities—what challenges do you think you face? How will you overcome these? How well developed are collaborative practices within your school?	From the answers to these questions you should be able to judge the growth state of the school, its performance level and its capacity to collaborate (low, medium, high). You should also be able to judge the levels of support the school will need and how far you need to develop the skills of collaboration with the school before it enters into partnership with other schools.	In this box you will record the evidence you have used to make a diagnosis of the school and the agreement between yourself and the school about the levels of support and the extent of the school's involvement in the collaborative partnership.

(Continued)

129

Individual School	'Start Up Phase'	Assessment	Facilitator Aide Memoire
Data	Having established the school's broad priority it will be important to try and generate a precise question of enquiry that the school wishes to pursue linked to its main priority. This way you should be able to create a more precise focus or set of foci among your schools so they can work together more productively. So you may want to probe further: Questions to ask: What data will you use to inform your focus of enquiry? What baseline data will you use to gauge the progress made relating to your question of enquiry? How will you measure or gauge the overall impact on learner outcomes; professional learning; organisational change? What will you use to monitor interim progress?	Broad statements of intent are not precise questions of enquiry. So the school may identify a problem with literacy but you need to push them to identify a particular issue or problem that could be a focus for enquiry by drilling down further in the data. So it could be that by looking at diagnostic assessments the school could identify a precise problem (e.g. reading for meaning) with a particular group (year 8 boys). This precision means that the issue is more manageable as a focus of enquiry as it is specific and measurable.	Note the question of enquiry and the data sets that they propose to use.

Development	Having make a diagnosis and prompted the school to be explicit about a question of enquiry, the next step is to think about the best mode of collaboration that could help that specific school. Gauge their experience in collaborative models first before drawing any conclusions.	This needs to be thought about for all your schools first before embarking upon a particular collaborative course. It may be that there has to be some compromise as the model might be ideal for the majority of schools but not all. This judgement is not shared with the school but is used by you as you make a decision about the collective approach you wish to use.	Record the extent of their experience with various approaches and their judgement of their success. This will help you to gauge experience in collaborative ways of working.
	Questions to ask:		
	Have you ever used any specific approaches to collaboration in your school (prompt PLC, Action Learning Sets, Learning Walks, etc)		
	How effective did you find the approaches you used? What worked, what didn't?	Note if the answer is that they have not tried anything specific then you need to explain a few of the potential approaches so they are totally clear about the nature of the collaborative partnership and to inform them of the available options.	

(Continued)

(Continued)

Individual School	'Start Up Phase'	Assessment	Facilitator Aide Memoire
Distributed Leadership	To work effectively as a collaborative team will require an understanding of distributed leadership where different members of the group at different times take on a leadership role. It is also important that the group understands that the 'facilitator' is not the formal leader of the group and is not going to play a dominant role. Questions to ask: How far is distributed leadership developed in this school? What experience do staff have of distributed leadership in action?	It is important that you gauge the extent to which the school and the individuals therein have direct experience of distributed leadership as this will influence how they work collaboratively. It will also affect how you work with the group initially as if there are some members who are not familiar with DL then the ground-rules will need to explicitly cover this aspect.	Note the experience of DL at different schools to assist you in your initial meeting with the individual members from each school.

| Drive | It is important to think about sustainability from the outset—initial enthusiasm may wane as workload increases or the novelty of collaboration wares [*sic*] off. It is important to impress upon the school and the individual that they need to think about ways of maintaining and supporting this collaborative activity over time.

Questions to ask:

What time and support will be given to the individual and the school group?

Is the collaborative activity part of the staff action plan linked to the school development?

How this is linked to monitoring and school self-evaluation? | The effectiveness of collaboration between schools depends upon their ability to stay the course and upon the support they get from the school. The more this activity is linked to the school's internal improvement processes the more likely it will be that this collaborative activity will be integral to the work of the school. | It is important to ascertain at the outset how far the collaborative efforts can be maintained and sustained. The commitment of the school and the individuals are essential if the collaborative effort is to result in positive outcomes. If these are not forthcoming then they will need to be highlighted, negotiated and fostered as the collaborative process unfolds. |

Phase Two—INNOVATION—Facilitator's Overview

Individual School	Action Phase	Facilitator's Assessment	Facilitator Aide Memoire
Diagnosis	In this phase you will need to work with your schools to support them through the process of enquiring, trialling and refining their strategies. Questions to ask: To what extent is the strategy working? What have been its strengths and weaknesses?	From the answers to these questions you should be able to judge the progress made and the changes in practice undertaken. You should also be able to judge the degree of progress made and how far you need to support their thinking about how to refine the strategies used.	In this box you should record what has been achieved along with an assessment (from the group) of the strengths and weaknesses of the strategies used. You need to also ascertain the group's next steps.

Data	In terms of judging the impact of the strategy used it will be important to ascertain what data has been used. Questions to ask: What interim data have you used/collected to inform your judgement about the effectiveness of the strategy?	It will be important to reinforce the importance of data to form judgements. Subjective judgements are fine but some independent (student or other) data will be required to qualify how far the strategy worked/did not work.	Make a note of the data that is being used to make the judgement. If no data or inappropriate data is forthcoming then you will need to return to the original data from the first meeting to determine the distance travelled.
Development	It is important that schools go through several cycles of trialling and refining so that superficial conclusions are not reached and the process of innovation is grounded in practice rather than a 'bolt on'. Questions to ask: How do you plan to embed these strategies or develop these strategies further? How do you intend to promote these strategies to others?	This development stage is crucial because it is the hard graft; it is where the real work of collaboration takes place. It is here that the strategies agreed by the collaborative group are put into practice. Therefore you will need to decide how far the strategies have been deployed effectively.	Record the group's collective views about the use of the strategies and how far they feel this work is changing practice. If the verdict is that it is not, then the group should be encouraged to think of other, more challenging strategies. The role of the facilitator in this phase is to challenge the group and to question how far their work both individually and collectively is really innovative and breaking new ground.

(Continued)

135

(Continued)

Individual School	Action Phase	Facilitator's Assessment	Facilitator Aide Memoire
Distributed Leadership	It is important that each member of the team contributes to the collaborative effort and has the opportunity to lead at different times. At each meeting it will be important to renegotiate roles and responsibilities so that leadership is shared. Questions to ask: Who is best placed to organise the group for the next meeting? Who will lead on the next phase of enquiry? Who will broker resources and support?	The facilitator will need to gauge how far individuals are fulfilling their roles and responsibilities and how well the group is functioning. The facilitator will need to assess the group's potential as well as the quality of collective working as there may be individuals getting in the way of progress. There may be a need for some intervention to keep the group on track at this stage and to judge how best to manage the situation with individuals.	Note how far the group are sharing responsibility. Are some group members dominant? Note what challenge and support is required to help the group keep going to achieve a positive outcome.
Drive	Through the process of innovation there will be inevitable peaks and troughs. The role of the facilitator is to keep momentum going and to ensure the group makes progress.	The facilitator will need to assess the individual/group progress or contribution and should be prepared to offer support or intervene if an individual/school is in need.	The facilitator needs to gauge each person's contribution to the original focus of enquiry and to the overall learning and progress of the group.

Data Collection

Method	Advantages	Limitations
INTERVIEWS To obtain information that would not easily be secured through other methods To compliment other methods	Allows for an in depth and direct response from various stakeholders eg [p]upils, teachers, parents, governors	Time consuming Analysis can prove difficult
QUESTIONNAIRES To obtain specific information and feedback from a larger number of respondents	Can provide both qualitative and quantitative data	Information collected may be of little value if insufficient time and thought has been given to questionnaire design and trialling The return rate can be low
ONLINE SURVEYS To obtain specific information and feedback from a larger number of respondents	Easy to set up and administer Very cost effective Data can be analysed instantly and remotely Results can be instantly shared and discussed via a cloud	Requires technical skill and IT expertise Time consuming and can be highly subjective
OBSERVATION To obtain data that cannot be collected using any other method eg skills, interaction, practice	Provides data and evidence that would be difficult to obtain by other means	

(Continued)

Method	Advantages	Limitations
AUDIO/VISUAL To obtain a complete and accurate record that can be easily shared and revisited	Can readily be shared with others A completely reliable and accurate record of the information provided Can be uploaded to a 'cloud' and widely accessed	Can be inhibitive and time consuming
LEARNING LOGS To obtain a progressive overview of individual or learning over time	Quick and easy to produce eg diary format Can be completed and shared online both individually or collectively	Relies heavily upon disciplined and continual commitment

One way of strengthening the validity of data is to employ more than one way of data collection method or to collect data from more than one set of respondents. This is known as triangulation. This does not mean that you will need three data collection methods or three types of informant just simply that different perspectives on the same issue are required. In addition, it is important to ensure that your data is reliable in the sense that there is consistency in the production of results. This would necessitate at least in principle another person being able to replicate the data collection and to achieve comparable evidence or results. Reliability is concerned with minimising the errors and biases that could occur when evaluating impact. So in summary you need to consider the following questions:

- Will the selected data collection methods actually collect what they are intended to collect (Validity)?
- How many different viewpoints are considered in evaluating impact and how are different perceptions captured (Triangulation)?
- If someone else were to collect the data using the same methods what would be the chances of obtaining similar results (Reliability)?

In an impact assessment it will be important to apply these three tests to the data, otherwise any data collected will be of dubious value and could be challenged.

Phase Three—IMPACT—Facilitator's Overview

Individual School	Action Phase	Assessment	Facilitator Aide Memoire
Diagnosis	In this phase you will need to encourage the group to reflect upon the original data and in so doing to gauge their individual and collective impact.	From the answers to these questions you should be able to assess the degree of impact and assess progress made.	In this box record the evidence of impact and any observations about the effectiveness of the group as a whole in achieving its objectives.
	Questions to ask:	You should also be able to judge how far the work of the group has influenced individual efforts and vice versa.	
	What evidence do you have to judge whether your innovative work has been successful or not?		
	What strategies were most/least effective? Why?		
	What would you do differently next time? Why?		

Data	It will be important to ascertain what data the individuals and group have used to gauge the impact of their efforts at 3 levels a) learners b) professionals c) school(s)	The data should relate directly to the focus of enquiry and therefore the assessment of impact should be straightforward. If this is not the case it is worth reflecting upon and discussing with the group what other data sources could have been used.	Record the types of impact data provided by the group and make an overall judgement about the extent to which the collaborative effort has resulted in positive and meaningful outcomes for a) learners b) professionals, c) school(s)
	Also it will be important for the group to assess its own effectiveness.		Note the reflections on the impact at each of the three levels.
	Questions to ask:		
	How far has your work had an impact on a) learners b) you as a professional and others c) your school/other schools (s)		
	To what extent?		
	What is your evidence?		

(Continued)

(Continued)

Individual School	Action Phase	Assessment	Facilitator Aide Memoire
Development	The group needs to reflect upon the way it has worked together collaboratively. Questions to ask: How well did you work together as a group? What were the collective outcomes?	The group needs to honestly and accurately reflect upon the extent to which their collaborative work has made a difference, has had an impact and how this might be shared with other professionals and other schools.	Record the group's assessment of impact and note any data sets they have used to corroborate the impact of their work. In terms of development, the collective outcomes might be how the group wished to continue, whether it needs to enquire further or what advice it would give other groups.

| Distributed Leadership | As the group has come to the end of their work together consideration needs to be given to how well they shared the leadership responsibility within the group.

Questions to ask:

How far has leadership been distributed within this group?

Were their times when the group felt a lack of leadership? When and why?

What will the group take away from the experience of working in this reciprocal way? | In assessing the success or otherwise of the group it is important to look at how far leadership was properly distributed as this is a key component of collaborative learning and group success. | Note the group/facilitator's reflections on whether leadership was adequately shared or not and record how far they feel that this had a bearing on the outcome of their collaborative work. |
|---|---|---|---|

(Continued)

(Continued)

Individual School	Action Phase	Assessment	Facilitator Aide Memoire
Drive	It is important that the collaborative working is not an end point but a means to influencing the learning of others more widely. Questions to ask: How do you intend to share this work more widely? What are the group's plans for dissemination? What are the next steps?		

Implementation Phase

School to School Network

Data Informed Priority			Collaboration Process		
School	Group		School	Group	
A			A		
B			B		
C			C		
D			D		
Collective Question(s) of enquiry			Agreed strategy/approach to trial and refine		

Innovation Phase

School to School Network

Enquiry Informed Strategies/Approaches—Feedback		
School	Group	
A		
B		
C		
D		
Agreed next steps		

Impact Phase

School to School Network

	Student	Professional		School
		Teacher Reflection	Changes	
Outcomes				
A				
B				
C				
D				
Agreed Recommendations and Dissemination				

Collaborative Learning Overview
School to School Network

Implementation					Innovation				Impact		
Data Informed Priority		**Collaboration Process**			**Enquiry Informed Strategies/ Approaches— Feedback**		**Student**		**Professional**		**School**
School	Group	School	Group		School	Group	Outcomes		Teacher Reflection		Changes
A		A			A		A				
B		B			B		B				
C		C			C		C				
D		D			D		D				
Collective Question(s) of enquiry		Agreed strategy/ approach to trial and refine			Agreed next steps		Agreed Recommendations and Dissemination				

References

Ban Al-Ani, A. H., & Bligh, M. C. (2011). Collaborating with "virtual strangers": Towards developing a framework for leadership in distributed teams. *Leadership, 7*, 219–249.

Bell, L., Bolam, R., & Cubillo, L. (2003). *A systematic review of the impact of school headteachers and principals on student outcomes.* London: EPPI- Centre, Social Science Research Unit, Institute of Education.

Berry, B., Johnson, D., & Montgomery, D. (2005). The power of teacher leadership. *Educational Leadership, 62*(5), 56.

Bielaczyc, K., & Collins, A. (1999). Learning communities in classrooms: A reconceptualization of educational practice. In C. Reigeluth (Ed.), *Instructional-design theories and models* (Vol. 2, pp. 269–292). London, UK: Erlbaum.

Blase, J. and Blase, J. (2002) *Breaking the silence: Overcoming the problem of principal mistreatment of teachers.* Thousand Oaks, CA: Corwin.

Bolden, R., Petrov, G., & Gosling, J. (2009). Distributed leadership in higher education: Rhetoric and reality. *Educational Management Administration Leadership, 37*(2), 257–277.

Boyle. A. Tower Hamlets: A Case Study, unpublished.

Bryk A. & Schneider, B. (2002). Trust in schools: A core resource of school reform. USA: ASCD

Camburn, E., & Han, S. W. (2009). Investigating connections between distributed leadership and instructional change. In A. Harris (Ed.), *Distributed leadership: Different perspectives* (pp. 30–45). Dordrecht, Netherlands: Springer Press.

Carmichael, L. (1982). Leaders as learners: A possible dream. *Educational Leadership, 40*(1), 58–59.

Chapman, C., Lindsay, G., Muijs, D., Harris, A., Arweck, E., & Goodall, J. (2010). Governance, leadership and management in federations of schools. *School Effectiveness and School Improvement,* 22(1), 53–75.

Chapman, C. Armstrong, P. Harris, A Muijs, D. Reynolds, D and Sammons, P. (2012) *School effectiveness and improvement research, policy and practice: Challenging the orthodoxy?* London: Routledge.

Codingley, P. (2013) *The role of professional learning in determining the teaching profession's future.* Centre for Strategic Education, www .cse.edu.au

Cohen, D., & Prusak, L. (2001). *In good company: How social capital makes organizations work.* Boston: Harvard Business Press.

Collins, J., & Hansen, M. (2011). *Great by choice: Uncertainty, chaos and luck.* New York, NY: HarperCollins.

Collins, J.C. (2001) *Good to great.* New York: Harper Business Press

Corcoran, T. & Goertz, M. (1995). Instructional capacity and high performance schools. *Educational Researcher , 24*(9), 27–31.

Covey, S.M.R. (with Merrill, R. R.). (2008). *The speed of trust: The one thing that changes everything.* New York: Free Press.

Darling-Hammond, L. (1996). The quiet revolution: Rethinking teacher development. *Educational Leadership, 53*(6), 4–10.

Darling-Hammond, L. Chung Wei, R.Andre, A.Richardson, N and Opphanos, S (2009) Professional learning in the learning profession: A status report on teacher development in the US and abroad.   National Staff Development Council, Stanford University

Day, C. Jacobson, S. & Johansson, O. (2011). Leading organisational learning and capacity building. *In:* Ylimaki, R. and Jacobson, S., eds., US and cross-national policies, practices and preparation. 29–50. New York: Springer.

Day C., Sammons, P., Leithwood, K., Harris, A., & Hopkins, D. (2009). *The impact of leadership on pupil outcomes: Final Report.* London, UK: DCSF.

Department for Education and Skills. (2007). *Independent study into school leadership.* London, UK: Price Waterhouse Coopers.

Drucker, P. (1988). *The coming of the new organisation.* Boston, MA: Harvard Business Review.

Dufour, R. & Eaker, R. (1998). Professional learning communities at work: Best practices for enhancing student achievement. Bloomington, IN: Solution Tree.

DuFour, R., Dufour, R., & Eaker, B. (2009). New insights into professional learning communities at work. In M. Fullan (Ed.), *The challenge of change* (pp. 87–104). Thousand Oaks, CA: Corwin.

DuFour, R. Dufour, R. and Eaker, B. (2009) *New insights into professional learning communities at work* in Fullan, M (2009) *The challenge of change.* Thousand Oaks, CA: Corwin.

DuFour, R., Dufour, R., Eaker, B., & Karhanek, G. (2010). *Raising the bar and closing the gap: Whatever it takes.* Bloomington, IN: Solution Tree Press.

DuFour, R., & Eaker, R. E. (1998). *Professional learning communities at work: Best practices for enhancing student achievement.* Washington, DC: National Educational Service.

Elmore, R. F. (2002). *Bridging the gap between standards and achievement: The imperative for professional development in education.* Washington, DC: Albert Shanker Institute.

Fitzgerald, T. and Gunter, H. (2006), Teacher leadership? A new form of managerialism. *New Zealand Journal of Educational Leadership,* Vol. 21, No. 2, pp. 44–57

Fullan, M. (2009). *The challenge of change: Start school improvement now* (2nd ed.). Thousand Oaks, CA: Corwin.

Fullan, M. (2010a). *All systems go: The change imperative for whole system reform.* Thousand Oaks, CA: Corwin.

Fullan, M. (2010b). *Motion leadership.* Thousand Oaks, CA: Corwin.

Fullan, M. (2011a). *Choosing the wrong drivers for whole system reform* (Centre for Strategic Education Seminar Series Paper No. 24). Retrieved from http://www.michaelfullan.ca/media/13501655630.pdf

Fullan, M. (2011b). *The moral imperative realized.* Thousand Oaks, CA: Corwin.

Fullan, M 2012, (73) *Stratosphere.* Canada: Pearson Press

Goldenberg, C. (2004). *Successful school change: Creating settings to improve teaching and learning.* New York, NY: Teachers College Press.

Hadfield and Chapman (2009) *Leading school based networks.* London: Routledge

Hall, D. (2013). The strange case of the emergence of distributed leadership in schools in England. *Educational Review, 65,* 468–487.

Hallinger P., & Heck, R. (2009). Distributed leadership in schools: Does system policy make a difference? In A. Harris (Ed.), *Distributed leadership: Different perspectives* (pp. 34–56). Dordrecht, Netherlands: Springer Press.

Hargreaves, A. (2003). *Teaching in the knowledge society.* San Francisco, CA: Jossey-Bass.

Hargreaves, A., & Fink, D. (2009). Distributed leadership: Democracy or delivery? In A. Harris (Ed.), *Distributed leadership: Different perspectives* (pp. 101–124). Dordrecht, Netherlands: Springer Press.

Hargreaves, A., Harris, A., Boyle, A., Ghent, K., Goodall, J., Gurn, A., Stone Johnson, C. (2010). *Performance beyond expectations.* London, UK: National College for Leadership and Specialist Schools and Academies Trust.

Hargreaves, A & Fullan, M. (2012). *Professional capital: Transforming teaching in every school.* New York: Teachers College Press.

Hargreaves, A., & Shirley, D. (2009). *The fourth way: The inspiring future for educational change.* Thousand Oaks, CA: Corwin.

Hargreaves, A. & Shirley, D. (2012) *The global fourth way.* California: Corwin.

Hargreaves, D. (2010) *Creating a self improving system.* Nottingham: National College for School Leadership (NCSL)

Harris, A. (2008). *Distributed leadership: Developing tomorrow's leaders.* London, UK: Routledge.

Harris, A. (2009). *Distributed leadership: Different perspectives.* Dordrecht, Netherlands: Springer Press.

Harris, A. (ed) (2009). *Distributed school leadership.* Netherlands: Springer Press.

Harris, A. (2011a). Distributed leadership: Current evidence and future directions. *Journal of Management Development, 30*(10), 20–32.

Harris, A. (2011b). System improvement through collective capacity building. *Journal of Educational Administration, 49*(6), 624–636.

Harris, A., & Jones, M. (2010). Professional learning communities and system improvement. *Improving Schools, 13*(2), 172–181.

Harris, A., & Jones, M. (2011). *Professional learning communities in action.* London, UK: Leannta Press.

Harris, A., & Jones, M. (2012). *Connecting professional learning.* Nottingham, UK: National College for School Leadership.

Harris, A., & Muijs, D. (2004). *Improving schools through teacher leadership.* London, UK: Oxford University Press.

Harris, A (2010) Leading system transformation, *School leadership and management* Vol 30 No 3 pages 197–209

Harris, A (2012) Leading system wide improvement; *International journal of leadership in education,* on line 28th February 2012

Harris, A (2013) Distributed leadership; friend or foe? *Educational management and administration* 41 (5) p 545–554

Harris, A. and Chrispeels J. (eds) (2006) *International perspectives on school improvement.* London: Routledge

Harris, A., Jones, M., Sharma, S. and Kannan, S (2013) Leading educational transformation in *Asia: Sustaining the knowledge society Asia Pacific journal of education* Vol 33 Issue 2 p 212–221

Hartley, D. (2010). Paradigms: How far does research in distributed leadership 'stretch'? *Educational Management, Administration and Leadership, 38,* 271–285.

Hartley, D. (2010) Paradigms: How far does research in distributed leadership 'stretch'? *Educational management, administration and leadership 38: 271–285*

Heck, R and Hallinger, P (2010). Testing a longitudinal model of distributed leadership effects on school improvement. *Leadership quarterly,* 21, 867–885

Heifetz, R. (1994). *Leadership without easy answers.* Cambridge, MA: Belknap Press.

Hopkins. D (2002) *Improving the quality of education for all.* London: David Fulton Press

Hopkins, D., & Jackson, D. (2003). Building the capacity for leading and learning. In A. Harris, C. Day, M. Hadfield, D. Hopkins, A. Hargreaves, & C. Chapman (Eds.), *Effective leadership for school Improvement* (pp. 84–104). London, UK: Routledge Falmer.

Hord, S. M. (1997). *Professional learning communities: Communities of continuous inquiry and improvement.* Austin, TX: Southwest Educational Development Laboratory.

Horton, J and Martin,   (2013) The role of districts in professional learning communities *International Journal of Leadership in Education: Theory and Practice, 16* (1)55–70.

Huffman, J. B., & Jacobson, A. L. (2003). Perceptions of professional learning communities. *International Journal of Leadership in Education: Theory and Practice, 6*(3), 239–250.

Hutchins, E. T. (1995). *Cognition in the wild.* Cambridge, MA: MIT.

Jensen, B. (2012). Catching up: Learning from the best school systems. In A. Hunter, J. Sonnemann, & Burns (Eds.), *Asia.* Victoria, Australia: Grattan Institute.

Johnson & Johnson (2010). *Where good ideas come from.* London: Penguin.

Jones, M. (2013) *Connect to learn: Learn to connect—Disciplined collaboration with impact.* University of Malaya Press

Kruger, M. (2009). The big five of school leadership competences in the Netherlands. *School Leadership and Management, 29*(2), 109–127.

Lave, J. & Wenger,E. (1991). *Situated learning: legitimate peripheral participation.* Cambridge: Cambridge University Press.

Leana, C.R. (2011) The missing link in school reform. *Stanford Social Innovation Review,* Stanford University.

Leithwood, K., & Jantzi, D. (2000). The effects of different sources of leadership on student engagement in school. In K. Riley & K. Louis

(Eds.), *Leadership for change and school reform* (pp. 50–66). London, UK: Routledge.

Leithwood, K., & Mascall, B. (2008). Collective leadership effects on student achievement. *Educational Administration Quarterly, 44*(4), 529–561.

Leithwood, K. Harris, A and Hopkins, D (2008) Seven strong claims about successful school leadership, *School leadership and management* 28 (1) 221–58.

Leithwood, K. Mascall, B. and Strauss, T. (2009) *Distributed leadership according to the evidence.* London: Routledge

Leithwood, K., Mascall, B., & Strauss, T. (2009). *Distributed leadership according to the evidence.* London, UK: Routledge.

Leithwood, K., Mascall, B., Strauss, T., Sacks, R., Memon, N., & Yashkina. (2009). Distributing leadership to make schools smarter: Taking the ego out of the system. In K. Leithwood, B. Mascall, & T. Strauss (Eds.), *Distributed leadership according to the evidence* (pp. 223–252). London, UK: Routledge.

Leithwood, K. Harris, A. Strauss, T. (2010) *Leading school turnaround.* San Francisco: Jossey Bass

Lemke, C. (2009). *Policy brief; Teacher learning through collaboration and system innovation.* Indianapolis, IN: Metri Group, Cisco.

Lewis, M., & Andrews, D. (2004). Building sustainable futures: Emerging understandings of the significant contribution of the professional learning community. *Improving Schools, 7*(2), 129–150.

Lieberman, A. (2009) Inquiring teachers: Making experience and knowledge public *Teachers College Record,* 111(8)1876–1881

Little, J. W. (1990). The persistence of privacy: Autonomy and initiative in teachers' professional relations. *Teachers college record* 91: 50–536.

Lumby, J. and Coleman, M (2007) *Leadership and diversity.* London: Sage

Lumby, J. (2013). Distributed leadership: The uses and abuses of power. *Educational Management Administration & Leadership, 41*(5/6).

Malaysian Blueprint 2013-2025. Ministry of Education, Malaysia.

Mitchell, C., & Learmond, D. (2010). Go where there be dragons: Leadership essentials for 2020 and beyond. The Conference Board Inc.

Møller, J., Eggen, A., Fuglestad, O. L., Langfeldt, G., Presthus, A., Skrøvset, S., . . . Vedoy, G. (2005). *Journal of Educational Administration, 43*(6), 584–594.

Morrissey, M. (2000). Professional learning communities: An ongoing exploration. Austin, TX: Southwest Educational Development Laboratory. Retrieved from http://allthingsplc .info/pdf/articles/plc-ongoing.pdf

Mourshed, M., & Barber, M. (2007). *How the world's best-performing schools come out on top.* London, UK: McKinsey.

Mourshed, M., Chijioke, C., & Barber, M. (2010). *How the world's most improved school systems keep getting better.* New York, NY: McKinsey.

Murphy, J., & Beck, L. (1995). *School-based management as school reform.* Thousand Oaks, CA: Corwin.

Murphy, J., Smylie, M., & Seashore Louis, K. (2009). The role of the principal in fostering the development of distributed leadership. *School Leadership and Management, 23,* 9.

National Institute of Education. (2011) *Leaders in education programme 2011—Handbook for participants.* Singapore: National Institute of Education Singapore.

Payne, C. (2008). *So much reform, so little change: The persistence of failure in urban schools.* Cambridge, MA: Harvard Education Press.

Polka, W.S. & Litchka, P.R. (2008). The dark side of educational leadership: superintendents and the professional victim syndrome. New York: Rowman & Littlefield.

Preece, J. (2002) Supporting community and building social capital. *Association for computing machinery.* Communications of the ACM (45:4) p 37.

Prusak, L., & Cohen, D. (2001). *In good company: How social capital makes organisations work.* Boston, MA: Harvard Business Press.

Riccii, R. Wiese, (2011). *Collaboration imperative executive strategies for unlocking your organization's true potential.* San Jose, CA: Cisco Systems.

Robinson, VMJ Lloyd, CA and Rowe KJ (2008), The impact of leadership on student outcomes: An analysis of the differential effects of leadership types *Educational administration quarterly* (EAQ). Vol. 44, No. 5, pp. 635–674

Sahlberg, P. (2011) *Finnish lessons.* Columbia University: Teachers College Press

Sammons, P., Mujtaba, T., Earl, L., & Gu, Q. (2007). Participation in network learning community programmes and standards of pupil achievement: Does it make a difference? *School Leadership and Management, 27*(3), 213–238.

Sargent, T. C., & Hannum, E. (2009). Doing more with less: Teacher professional learning communities in resource-constrained primary schools in rural China. *Journal of Teacher Education, 60*(3), 258–276.

Saunders, W., & Goldenberg, C. (2005). The contribution of settings to school improvement and school change. In C. O'Donnell & L. Yamauchi (Eds.), *Culture and context in human behaviour change: Theory, research and applications* (pp. 127–150). New York, NY: Peter Lang.

Saunders, W., Goldenberg, C., & Gallimore, R. (2009). Increasing achievement by focusing grade level teams on improving classroom learning: A prospective quasi-experimental study of Title 1 schools. *American Educational Research Journal, 46,* 1006–1013.

Scribner, J. P., Sawyer, K., Watson, S. T., & Myers, V. L. (2007). Discourse and collaboration teacher teams and distributed leadership: A study of group. *Educational Administration Quarterly, 43,* 67–100.

Senge, P. (1990). *The fifth discipline.* New York, NY: Doubleday.

Sharrat, L., & Fullan, M. (2009). *Realization: The change imperative for deepening district wide reform.* Thousand Oaks, CA: Corwin.

Silns, H. & Mulford, B. (2002). Leadership and school results. *Second International Handbook of Educational Leadership and Administration,* Netherlands: Springer Press.

Spillane, J. P. (2006) *Distributed leadership.* San Francisco, CA: Jossey-Bass.

Spillane, J. P., & Camburn, E. (2006, April). *The practice of leading and managing: The distribution of responsibility for leadership and management in the schoolhouse.* Paper presented at the annual meeting of the American Educational Research Association, San Francisco, CA.

Spillane, J. P., & Coldren, A. F. (2011). *Diagnosis and design for school improvement.* New York, NY: Teachers College Press.

Spillane, J. P., & Diamond, J. B. (2007). A distributed perspective *on* and *in* practice. In J. P. Spillane & J. B. Diamond (Eds.), *Distributed leadership in practice* (pp. 146–166). New York, NY: Teachers College Press.

Spillane, J. P., Halverson, R., & Diamond, J. B. (2001a). Investigating school leadership practice: A distributed perspective. *Educational Researcher, 30*(3), 23–28.

Spillane, J., Halverson, R., & Diamond, J. (2001b). *Towards a theory of leadership practice: A distributed perspectiv*e (Working paper). Evanston, IL: Northwestern University, Institute for Policy Research.

Spillane, J.P., Parise, L.M. & Sherer, J.Z. (2011) Organizational routines as coupling mechanisms: Policy, school administration, and the technical core. *American educational research journal*: 48(3): 586–620.

Stoll, L. (2012). Stimulating learning conversations. *Professional Development Today, 14*(4), 6–12.

Stoll, L., Bolam, R., McMahon, A., Wallace, M., & Thomas, S. (2006). Professional learning communities: A review of the literature. *Journal of Educational Change, 7*(4), 221–258.

Stoll, L., & Seashore Louis, K. (Eds.). (2007). *Professional learning communities.* Maidenhead, UK: Open University Press.

Surowiecki, J. (2005). *The wisdom of crowds.* New York, NY: Random House.

Timperley, H. (2005). Distributed leadership: Developing theory from practice. *Journal of Curriculum Studies, 37*(4), 395–420.

Timperley, H. Wilson, A. Barrar, H and Fung, I (2007) *Teacher professional learning and development: Best evidence synthesis.* University of Auckland, New Zealand.

Verscio, V., Ross, D., & Adams, A. (2008). A review of research on the impact of professional learning communities on teaching practice and student learning. *Teaching and Teacher Education, 21,* 80–91.

Waters, T. & Cameron, G. (2003). *The balanced leadership framework, Connecting vision with action.* Denver, CO: Mid-continent Research for Education and Learning.

Waters, T., & Cameron, G. (2007). *The balanced leadership framework.* Denver, CO: McREL. Retrieved from http://ok.gov/sde/sites/ok.gov.sde/files/TLE-FrameworkBooklet.pdf

Weick, K. E. (2001). *Making sense of the organization.* Oxford, UK: Blackwell.

Weick, K. E. (2001). The collapse of sensemaking in organizations: The Mann gulch disaster. *Administrative Science Quarterly, 38,* 347.

Wenger, E. (2000). Communities *of practice and social learning systems, Organization, 7*(2), 225–246.

Whelan, F. (2009). *Lessons learned: How good policies produce better schools.* Bodmin, UK: MPG Books.

Whitehurst, G. J. (2002). *Research on teacher preparation and professional development.* Paper presented at the White House Conference on Preparing Tomorrow's Teachers, Washington, DC.

Wilkson, J and Pickett, K (2009) *The spirit level—Why greater equality makes societies stronger.* London: Bloomsbury Press

World Bank. (1999). *World Development Report 1998/1999: Knowledge for development.* New York, NY: Oxford University Press.

Wright, L. (2008). Merits and limitations of distributed leadership: Experiences and understandings of school principals. *Canadian Journal of Educational Administration and Policy*, (69) 1–33.

Youngs, H. (2009). (Un) Critical times? Situating distributed leadership in the field. *Journal of Educational Administration and History*, *41*, 377–389.

Yukl, G. (2002). *Leadership in organizations* (5th ed.). Upper Saddle, NJ: Prentice Hall.

Index

CORWIN

A SAGE Company